"In *Social Anxiety Relief for Teens*, Bridget Flynn Walker provides all the tools kids need to start recognizing, challenging, and overcoming their social anxiety. If your life feels limited or miserable because of social anxiety, give this book a try. If you know a young person who is struggling with social anxiety, encourage them to follow the clear, simple, and easy-to-understand steps laid out in this excellent volume."

—**Eli R. Lebowitz, PhD**, director of the Yale Child Study Center Program for Anxiety Disorders, and author of *Breaking Free of Child Anxiety and OCD*

"Social anxiety is very common, and it can really hold you back. This can be a really big problem when you are teenager. Fortunately, there are very effective skills to deal with this problem. This book is a step-by-step guide to manage and overcome this problem. Don't suffer in silence. There is a way out. This book will help you."

—**Stefan G. Hofmann, PhD**, professor at Boston University, and author of *The Anxiety Skills Workbook*

"This workbook is an excellent tool for teenagers struggling with social anxiety. Bridget Flynn Walker provides a stepwise and structured plan, rooted in scientific evidence, to help teens guide themselves through the process of understanding the nature of their social anxiety. The vignettes and FAQs really make the content of the book come to life. The content around exposures, which are the heart of the book, is well explained and easy to understand. I am going to definitely use this book with patients."

—**Rachel Busman, PsyD, ABPP**, clinical psychologist, and senior director of the Child and Adolescent Anxiety & Related Disorders Center at Cognitive and Behavioral Consultants

"In clear, direct, relatable language, Bridget Flynn Walker has followed up her acclaimed book for parents of anxious kids with an indispensable guide for teens with social anxiety. The practical, step-by-step approach is grounded in the most current research and reads like your wisest relative encouraging you along the way. I hope my pediatrician colleagues place copies in their waiting rooms!"

—**David Becker, MD, LMFT**, clinical professor in the department of pediatrics at the University of California, San Francisco

"In clear, teen-friendly language, Bridget Flynn Walker's *Social Anxiety Relief for Teens* walks the socially anxious teen step-by-step down a cognitive behavior therapy (CBT) path toward more successful social engagement. As soon as I read it, I thought of several kids to whom I must get this book!"

—**Margo Thienemann, MD**, clinical professor of psychiatry at Stanford University, and cofounder and lead psychiatrist at the Immune Behavioral Health Clinic at Stanford Children's Health

"Now more than ever, this accessible and practical guide is a must-read for any adolescent suffering from social anxiety, as well as any adult in their life. It simultaneously honors the whole person and their experience, all while giving concrete and achievable steps toward healing. Bridget Flynn Walker is gifted at reaching teenagers where they're at, and this text is a reflection of her gifts."

—**Katie Blaesing**, counselor and anti-bias education coordinator at The Hamlin School

"Both pithy and thorough, Bridget Flynn Walker carefully explains what social anxiety is, how avoidance and safety behaviors maintain social anxiety, and how teens can cope with and overcome social anxiety. While covering typical and more taboo aspects of social anxiety, Walker never blames or shames teens for being anxious. This amazing book talks directly to socially anxious teens in a way that is clear, direct, and relatable."

—**Daniela Owen, PhD**, assistant director of the San Francisco Bay Area Center for Cognitive Therapy; and author of *Right Now, I Am Fine*

"Just in time, in a world awash in overwhelming worries, here is a clear and straightforward guide on how to master social phobias. Bridget Flynn Walker's prescriptive, step-by-step instructions provide the tools to successfully navigate stressful social situations. If you or your teen is struggling with anxiety and you are ready to take it on, this is the book for you."

—**Laurel Schultz, MD, MPH**, community pediatrician at Golden Gate Pediatrics in San Francisco, CA

the *instant* help solutions series

Young people today need mental health resources more than ever. That's why New Harbinger created the **Instant Help Solutions Series** especially for teens. Written by leading psychologists, physicians, and professionals, these evidence-based self-help books offer practical tips and strategies for dealing with a variety of mental health issues and life challenges teens face, such as depression, anxiety, bullying, eating disorders, trauma, and self-esteem problems.

Studies have shown that young people who learn healthy coping skills early on are better able to navigate problems later in life. Engaging and easy-to-use, these books provide teens with the tools they need to thrive—at home, at school, and on into adulthood.

This series is part of the **New Harbinger Instant Help Books** imprint, founded by renowned child psychologist Lawrence Shapiro. For a complete list of books in this series, visit newharbinger.com.

social anxiety relief for teens

a step-by-step cbt guide to **feel confident** & **comfortable** in any **situation**

BRIDGET FLYNN WALKER, PhD

Instant Help Books
An Imprint of New Harbinger Publications, Inc.

Publisher's Note

This publication is designed to provide accurate and authoritative information in regard to the subject matter covered. It is sold with the understanding that the publisher is not engaged in rendering psychological, financial, legal, or other professional services. If expert assistance or counseling is needed, the services of a competent professional should be sought.

INSTANT HELP and the Clock Logo are registered trademarks of New Harbinger Publications, Inc.

Distributed in Canada by Raincoast Books

Copyright © 2021 by Bridget Flynn Walker
Instant Help Books
An imprint of New Harbinger Publications, Inc.
5674 Shattuck Avenue
Oakland, CA 94609
www.newharbinger.com

Cover design by Amy Shoup; Acquired by Jennye Garibaldi; Edited by Marisa Solis

All Rights Reserved

Library of Congress Cataloging-in-Publication Data

Names: Walker, Bridget Flynn, author. | Tompkins, Michael A., author.
Title: Social anxiety relief for teens : a step-by-step CBT guide to feel confident and comfortable in any situation / by Bridget F. Walker, PhD. Michael A. Tompkins.
Description: Oakland, CA : New Harbinger Publications, [2021] | Includes bibliographical references.
Identifiers: LCCN 2021007019 | ISBN 9781684037056 (trade paperback)
Subjects: LCSH: Social phobia in adolescence--Juvenile literature. | Social phobia in adolescence--Treatment--Juvenile literature. | Anxiety in adolescence--Juvenile literature. | Cognitive therapy--Juvenile literature.
Classification: LCC RJ506.S63 W35 2021 | DDC 618.92/85225--dc23
LC record available at https://lccn.loc.gov/2021007019

Printed in the United States of America

24	23	22					
10	9	8	7	6	5	4	3

Contents

	Foreword	vii
Chapter 1	The Many Faces of Social Anxiety	1
Chapter 2	Knowledge Is Power	15
Chapter 3	Your CBT Toolbox	29
Chapter 4	Creating a Trigger Situations List	41
Chapter 5	Identifying Avoidance and Safety Behaviors	59
Chapter 6	Building an Exposure Ladder	77
Chapter 7	Drilling Down on Your Fear	99
Chapter 8	Planning an Exposure Experiment	113
Chapter 9	Running an Exposure Experiment	129
Chapter 10	Getting the Most from Your Exposures	143
Chapter 11	How Well Are You Doing?	163
	Resources	173
	References	175

I wondered how many people there were in the world who suffered, and continued to suffer, because they could not break out from their own web of shyness and reserve, and in their blindness and folly built up a great distorted wall in front of them that hid the truth. This is what I had done. I had built up false pictures in my mind and sat before them. I had never had the courage to demand the truth. Had I made one step forward out of my own shyness...

—Daphne du Maurier, *Rebecca*

Foreword

Do you feel anxious when you're around people? Do you worry that people don't like you? Are you convinced people think you're weird? Do you sweat, shake, or feel nauseous when you're asked to give a report in front of a class or when you perform in a sport? Will you do anything to avoid talking to people you don't know well? Do you avoid going to a party or out on a date? Do you even avoid looking people in the eye, or saying hello to people you know? If any or all of these ring true for you, you'll want to try the program that is described in this book.

Dr. Bridget Flynn Walker is a clinical psychologist who has worked for many years with teens who suffer from different types of anxiety. I'm thrilled that she has now put the methods she uses successfully in her office into this book, which deals specifically with social anxiety. You can work with this book on your own, or you can use it with the assistance of your therapist or counselor. In this book, Dr. Walker guides you through the cognitive behavioral therapy (CBT) program she has tailored for teens. She lays it out step by step and answers many of the questions you may have about social anxiety and this program.

Perhaps you've avoided doing anything about your social anxiety because you didn't think there was anything that could help. Or perhaps you're too embarrassed to seek help. Or perhaps you sought support in the past, but it wasn't helpful. I realize that asking for help or even letting others know how much you're suffering can be difficult. In fact, making it over this initial hurdle can be the hardest part. But if you've read this far, you likely have the drive, the grit, and the motivation to overcome your social anxiety. I strongly encourage you to give it a try! Honestly, I think it's fair to say that you've nothing to lose and everything to gain.

—Michael A. Tompkins, PhD, ABPP
Author of *My Anxious Mind: A Teen's Guide to Managing Anxiety and Panic*

CHAPTER 1

The Many Faces of Social Anxiety

The most stressful part of the school day for Steffie, a high school sophomore, is lunch. She usually eats with the same two best friends, Lola and Abby. When her BFFs are busy, or if they want to include kids Steffie doesn't know well, she goes to the library to avoid the uncomfortable situation. She might make the excuse that she has schoolwork to do, even if she has none.

But today it's just the three girls at their favorite table in the corner of the cafeteria.

"You'd better come with us this time!" Lola says as soon as Steffie sits down.

"Where?"

"The pizza party at Elliott's on Saturday," Abby says. "It's going to be supercool."

"Yeah," Lola echoes. "You didn't go last time. And you know how much we want you with us!"

When Steffie hesitates, Lola says, "You do want to be with us, don't you?"

"Of course," Steffie says, though she can feel her heart starting to pound and that familiar panicky feeling rising in her stomach.

She's not lying to her friends: she does want to go. Elliott's mom made awesome pizza for a charity fundraiser at school. And Elliott's pretty cool himself. But then Steffie thinks about what it will be like standing around at the party and trying to make chitchat. That terrifies her.

When Saturday rolls around, Steffie gets a text confirming Lola and her mom will pick her up for the party. Steffie texts back, "okay," but wishes she hadn't let her friends think she'd go. She's really not up to it. Except she's afraid they'll think she's dumb—or worse, a crappy friend—if she backs out now. So she tells herself she can handle this. If it turns out she can't, well, then she'll just leave early.

Steffie gets dressed and goes out to the front porch to wait for Lola and her mom. As she stands there, she's flooded with anxiety. Her thoughts go to the worst possible scenarios: *The kids will wonder what I'm doing there. I won't be able to talk. They'll notice I'm super nervous and think I'm crazy. I'll absolutely die at that party!* She starts to shake and sweat and become so nauseated that she feels ready to vomit.

She picks up her phone and texts Lola: "Sorry. I'm sick. Can't make it tonight."

Lola texts back a frowny face and "feel better."

Steffie thinks she detects sarcasm in that "feel better." It's what Lola said the last time Steffie flaked. As she goes inside, Steffie is very disappointed in herself. She's ashamed to be so fearful of a situation that other kids have no problem with. But she doesn't know how to fix this.

"What happened, hun?" asks Steffie's mom in surprise. "I thought you were going to the party?"

Steffie doesn't have a way to explain herself. She runs upstairs, locks herself in her room, and refuses to speak to her parents for the remainder of the night. She dreads facing Lola and Abby at school on Monday and wonders what they may have said to others about her absence at the party.

WHAT IS SOCIAL ANXIETY?

Steffie is suffering from *social anxiety*. What does that mean? In simple terms, social anxiety involves feeling extreme worry and fear related to social situations. That worry and fear typically focus on feeling judged, being negatively evaluated, or being rejected by others.

Social anxiety has many faces. For Steffie, anxiety means avoiding kids she doesn't know well. For someone else, it might mean being a total loner. Yet another person with social anxiety might constantly seek reassurance from parents or others, even to the point of appearing clingy. As different as these faces may seem on the outside, the anxiety beneath the surface and the continual monitoring of situations are likely quite similar. It's hard to relax with friends or act natural in a classroom when the mind's internal processor is going a mile a minute.

Because we all tend to place special importance during our teen years on what others think of us, getting extra worried about that can seem like really bad timing. It can make days at school feel like a minefield. Everywhere you turn, you see reasons to worry that others don't like you, don't want to talk to you, or think you aren't pretty or handsome or smart or cool enough. Other people probably don't actually think or feel those things at all, but you can't shake the belief that they do.

In fact, the things you do to avoid people's judgment can result in judgment where there otherwise would be none. For example, always avoiding eye contact can make you look sketchy or stuck up. If you prepare topics of conversation ahead of time so as not to sound boring, you can end up sounding artificial or stiff. Wearing lots of makeup to cover signs of blushing can make you look out of place. In these and other ways, social anxiety becomes a self-fulfilling prophecy.

The good news is that you can stop the vicious cycle and conquer your anxiety. In this book, I'm going to introduce you to a program to do exactly that, and I'll walk you through the steps. However, first let's get a better sense of how social anxiety functions and whether you are experiencing it.

Why Do So Many Teens Have Social Anxiety?

Since the days of cave dwellers, humans have been social animals. Learning to live with others is a natural part of each person's development. The teen years, in particular, are a time of big change. Not only is your body undergoing amazing physical changes, but you're also growing socially.

You are branching out from your family in new ways and spending more time with your peers. Instead of looking mainly to your parents for guidance, you have many new influences in your life. Your world is expanding, and you're becoming more independent.

Your psyche is also developing in new ways. As a teen, you're more aware of your inner thoughts and feelings. At the same time, you're more aware of how you are perceived by others. You notice what others are wearing, how they speak, what they value. All this further expands your world.

As exciting as all these changes are, they can also bring increased anxiety. Life is a lot more complex in today's world than it was for cave dwellers. And so, as you strive to make friends and be accepted into new social groups, there are more reasons to experience anxiety. This anxiety may be severe enough to cause a lot of distress and get in the way of forming friendships. Or it can be less severe yet still cause you to feel uncomfortable around others, both in and out of school.

If what you are reading here about social anxiety sounds similar to your experience, you're not alone. It is normal for teens to have a degree of social anxiety. However, for some, this normal nervousness is more persistent. It is estimated that as many as 10 percent of teens experience ongoing distress from social anxiety. Whether your anxiety is mild or more persistent, the program in this book should be helpful for you.

What Causes Social Anxiety

Unfortunately, we can't pinpoint a single cause for social anxiety. However, we do know it runs in families. If your parents or other relatives have any form of anxiety, you may as well. Your genetics may make your brain pay more attention to socially threatening information. Your brain may also be more likely to interpret neutral situations as threatening even when there is no real threat. To add to this problem, your brain may miss information that would signal there's nothing to worry about. The result is a lot of worry and fear and anxiety in social situations, because you believe actual harm will come to you.

Some scientists are researching which chemicals in the body might contribute to social anxiety, but more research is needed to get a clear picture. In the meantime, the important thing to remember is that you haven't done anything wrong. None of this is your fault!

DO YOU HAVE SOCIAL ANXIETY?

While not everyone's experiences of social anxiety are identical, there are common elements. These include physical sensations, disturbing and often repetitive thoughts, specific situations that are hard to handle, and how we react.

The following list covers many of these elements. To see if you might suffer from social anxiety, check all the statements that are true for you either sometimes (1) or often (2). Don't check statements that are not true for you.

	1 (sometimes)	2 (often)
1. I feel these sensations when I'm with others:		
• Shaking or trembling		
• Heart pounding		
• Sweating		
• Muscle tension		
• Excessive blushing		
• Feeling out of breath		
• Dizziness		
• Nausea		
• Vomiting		
• Blank mind		
2. I have these thoughts about being with others:		
• *They think I'm weird.*		
• *They think I'm not good enough.*		
• *They won't like me.*		
• *They'll talk about me behind my back.*		
• *I am weird* [or *stupid* or *ugly* or any other judgment].		
• *I am not good enough.*		
• *I'll be embarrassed.*		

• I'll offend or hurt others.		
• I'll inconvenience others.		
3. I don't like situations that involve:		
• Talking with strangers		
• Raising my hand in class		
• Making a presentation in class		
• Being the last person to arrive in a room or at an event		
• Attending a party		
• Going on a date		
• Making eye contact		
• Eating in front of others		
• Using a public restroom		
4. I respond to uncomfortable situations with others by:		
• Hanging only with kids I know well		
• Avoiding situations with kids I don't know well		
• Leaving the situation as quickly as possible		
• Wearing earbuds		
• Hiding my anxiety		
• Talking as little as possible		
• Feeling depressed about it		
• Asking my parents or teachers to accommodate me		
• Taking a drug or self-medicating		

If you have checked either 1 (sometimes) or 2 (often) for most items on this list, chances are you suffer from social anxiety. The items you experience often are especially important to look at, and you will have a chance to work with these in the chapters that follow. (Please note that this isn't an official test for social anxiety; it is just meant to give you a good sense of what you are experiencing.)

AVOIDANCE AND SAFETY BEHAVIORS

Social anxiety is an extremely unpleasant feeling. It may not even make sense to you, and others who see you experiencing it might not understand it either. What's scary about speaking in class, when others can do it? Everyone else seems happy when you sit down for lunch, so why not you?

You might actually feel ashamed of your social anxiety. So, on top of having to deal with the pangs of anxiety on a daily basis, you also have to deal with shame. Or you might feel downright depressed because of it. For all these reasons, it's natural to want to prevent yourself from feeling intense fear and anxiety.

The two main ways people commonly cope with social anxiety are by using avoidance behaviors and by using safety behaviors. *Avoidance behaviors* refer to any ways you try to avoid being in or thinking about a particular situation that triggers worry or fear. *Safety behaviors* refer to things you do (actions or thoughts) to make the feared consequence of being in a trigger situation less likely.

Before we discuss these behaviors in more detail, let's consider the experience of Martin, a high school senior. Martin attends a school with kids he's known for much of his life, but he keeps mostly to himself. He avoids raising his hand or speaking in class because he worries he'll go blank, shake, and turn red. The possibility of feeling embarrassed terrifies him. He is certain the other kids will think he's a freak.

Martin's parents took him to a pediatrician, who predicted Martin would "grow out" of his fears. But he hasn't. His anxiety doesn't extend to adults, including his teachers. Every year, he asks his teachers to make special accommodations. For example, when his World Politics teacher, Mrs. Chu, assigned an oral presentation, he asked to be excused.

Mrs. Chu was confused. "But you're so articulate when you're talking to me," she said. "I don't see why you're worried about the class. You have a lot to offer."

"I know I can do an A+ presentation," Martin said. "I just want to be able to present it the best way I can. Getting into a good college is important to me."

In the end, Mrs. Chu let Martin give his oral presentation privately. She said she knows he has mastered the material and she wants to do anything she can to help him.

Now Martin is completing applications for college. He had to endure school tours, including meeting college students. The way he got through it was by having his parents do the talking. His mother didn't object. In fact, she felt she was protecting her son. She reminded him that he would outgrow his discomfort.

"I'm sure you're going to love college," his mom said. "You're such a good student. The rest will come naturally."

Martin isn't so sure. He's really worried about how he will handle a roommate, eating in the dining commons, and being around so many kids his age. He is considering attending college online. His parents assure him that they're happy to have him stay home another year and start college online. However, that is not what Martin really wants for himself.

At a recent family wedding, Martin tried alcohol for the first time. He noticed he was less anxious talking to his cousins and other kids his age. In fact, he actually danced with a bunch of kids. After the wedding, he read a comment online by a teen with social anxiety who wrote that alcohol helps. So one recent morning before school, when his parents weren't looking, Martin poured himself a little drink. He hoped it would ease his nerves in class. *If this works,* he told himself, *it may be the key to handling my transition into college.*

Martin used a combination of avoidance and safety behaviors. Which ones did you notice? Here are a few. See if you can identify others.

Avoidance behaviors:

- Not socializing with other kids
- Not raising his hand in class
- Planning to attend college online
- Wanting to live at home after high school

Safety behaviors:

- Receiving reassurance that he'll "get over it"
- Getting permission to give private presentations to his teachers
- Having his parents talk for him on college tours
- Drinking alcohol at parties and at school

Notice that some of these safety behaviors involve not just Martin but also people acting as enablers. Martin's mother and Mrs. Chu thought they were helping Martin by keeping him safe. Their intentions may have been good, but they didn't realize their help was counterproductive.

That is the problem of using either avoidance or safety behaviors, or both: you may feel better when you do them because they seem to actually decrease your anxiety in that moment. You feel less anxious if you don't raise your hand, or don't go to that uncomfortable party, or let your mom protect you. However, don't let yourself be fooled! Those fixes don't provide a long-term solution. What feels good now is likely to feel worse later.

CAPTIVE TO ANXIETY

Juanita remembers that the last time she went to soccer practice some kids laughed when she tripped. She is certain they will laugh at her again, so she tells her mother she isn't going to practice today.

"If you go," her mother says, "maybe you'll have more fun this time—you know, all laugh together."

"No way, Mom," Juanita says. "I hate when kids laugh at me. It's not fun."

"I thought it was fun when you made that big goal," her mother prompts.

Juanita stops for a second. "Mom, do you really think I'll make another goal?"

"Of course you will!" her mother says.

But that still isn't enough for Juanita. She hasn't forgotten the laughter after she fell down in practice. Remembering it now, she feels panicked. So she digs in.

"Like I said, I'm not going."

In this way, avoidance and safety behaviors maintain and feed social anxiety. Juanita used the avoidance behavior of declining to go to practice. Her safety behavior was asking her mother's reassurance that she would make another goal. By zeroing in on memories of past failures, you stop yourself from risking another uncomfortable social situation. If you do take that risk, you still keep looking for evidence to support your dire predictions. Either way, you'll likely fail to notice any signs of approval, affection, or support others may extend to you. Instead, you let everything they do or say feed into your negative assumptions about yourself: "People think I'm stupid." "I always stutter." "I have to be funny all the time."

You (and your parents and friends) may try to use logic to reassure you there is no real threat: "People don't really think you're stupid." "You don't always stutter." "You don't have to be funny all the time." But mere logic doesn't have the power to break the cycle of anxiety. Even though we know in our wise minds that our fears are bigger than they need to be, our brains continue to get stuck and turn up the volume. All that mental confusion and intense emotion convinces us to believe our fears. So we continue avoidance and safety behaviors that make us feel less worried, and we remain trapped in the clutches of distress. It's like being held captive.

Not only does social anxiety make your life stressful now, but it can also affect your future. Studies show that untreated social anxiety tends to get worse over time. Avoidance leads to more avoidance. For example, if you don't look someone in the eye who says hi to you before school, it will be harder to look a second or third person in the eye at lunchtime. And these behaviors can extend into other situations. If, for instance, you let your parents talk for you while ordering at a restaurant today, you may need them to talk for you at a job interview next week. In this way, you build fear instead of overcoming it.

Untreated social anxiety can lead to depression. We saw the beginning of that with Steffie, when she hid in her room all weekend. It can also lead to substance abuse, as we saw with Martin, who turned to alcohol. Over time, untreated social anxiety can interfere with major life experiences, such as relationships, education, and career development. I can't tell you how many adults I've helped who turned down a job they would have loved and excelled at because it required public presentations.

I'm not trying to scare you with this information. But I do want you to think about your future. I want you to ask yourself the tough questions: *Do I want to overcome my anxiety? Do I want to work for a better future for myself? Am I willing to stop avoiding situations or creating safety for myself, and work toward a long-term solution?*

BREAKING FREE

You can break free from the mental jail of social anxiety. The program I share in this book uses the techniques of *cognitive behavioral therapy* (CBT). CBT is about learning how to use the power of your mind to change your behaviors. Changing your behaviors, in turn, retrains your brain so you don't have to experience anxiety in social situations.

I didn't personally invent the basics of the CBT Social Anxiety Relief Program or the theory behind it. Versions have been widely used for years and have been found to be very effective in helping people of all ages conquer their anxiety and other similar problems. This program is readily adaptable to changing circumstances. For example, the teens you'll meet in this book aren't doing social distancing or virtual learning. However, if you're experiencing social anxiety in those situations, you can apply the same principles and practices.

In the following chapter, I explain how the CBT Social Anxiety Relief Program works. Then I'll guide you, step by step, through the program in the remaining chapters. In a nutshell, you will no longer engage in avoidance and safety behaviors. Instead, you'll do experiments that gradually make your anxieties lose their power over you. Before you freak out at the sound of that—I know that the idea of facing your fears may be frightening—please read on to learn more about how the program works and how it has helped hundreds of teens just like you.

CHAPTER 2

Knowledge Is Power

In the previous chapter, you met three teens with social anxiety. Steffie was uncomfortable around anyone who wasn't a close friend. Martin was afraid of facing college life. Juanita was anxious on the soccer field, even though she excelled at the game. Each faced severe consequences from their anxiety. Steffie was at risk of cutting herself off from all social situations. Martin was on the verge of skipping out on his college plans. Juanita was about to quit the soccer team. Ultimately, none had to experience their most-feared negative outcomes. Instead, they followed the CBT Social Anxiety Relief Program to conquer their social anxiety. It required some effort, but it worked for each of them. And it most certainly can work for you, too, if you're willing to put in the effort.

In this chapter, we will preview the steps you will follow as you undertake the CBT Social Anxiety Relief Program for teens. Since you'll be called upon to become the expert on yourself in this process, you need to understand how anxiety is maintained and how CBT works to address it.

HOW CBT COMBATS ANXIETY

When you have social anxiety, your mind mistakenly interprets everyday social situations as dangerous or threatening. For example, suppose you walk by a classmate who's busy on their phone. When they don't smile at you, your anxious mind produces the same thoughts you'd have if they outright called you a loser. Based on this misinterpretation—and with no evidence to back it up—your mind makes dire and extreme predictions. Your mind might predict, for instance, that the classmate is texting terrible things about you to others. Based on false predictions, your mind makes misguided attempts to protect you. It might insist, for example, that you avoid all activities where this "threatening" classmate is present. Or your mind might prompt you to ask your friends whether you had done anything to offend the person. In short, your mind directs you to engage in avoidance and safety behaviors.

In this program, you will systematically test your predictions to see if they're true. In this way, you'll work with your own mind to reduce the power it has over you.

THE TRAP OF AUTOMATIC THOUGHTS

Aaron Beck, the scientist who created cognitive therapy more than fifty years ago, understood that our thoughts drive how we feel in any given moment. A mind prone to anxiety creates thoughts that make situations seem dangerous in some way. It does this even in neutral situations that shouldn't set off alarm bells.

Dr. Beck called these kinds of distorted, negative, irrational thoughts *automatic thoughts*. These worry-thoughts are automatic because they pop up like a reflex. You automatically think, *They don't like me* or *They think I'm weird* or *I'm not good enough*. It's not that you want to think this way—you can't help it. It's like your brain runs away with you.

These thoughts take over your mind and, as a result, your behaviors. Even if you know logically that these thoughts don't make sense or that they distort what's happening, they have tremendous power over you. I like to call them *thinking errors*. Our brains can make all kinds of mistakes, and thinking errors are one kind. Individuals with social anxiety make different thinking errors. However, they all lead to the same result: they create anxiety.

To escape the anxiety caused by your thinking errors, it's tempting to engage in avoidance and safety behaviors. The problem is that this actually makes your anxiety worse. For example, think about Steffie during her lunch recess. She texts her BFFs about their lunch plans but doesn't hear back from either of them. She worries that if she goes to their usual hangout, the gym hallway, her BFFs won't be there. She takes a chance and heads there anyway. When she arrives, sure enough, no BFFs. A couple of seniors she doesn't know well are there. Instantly, her fear skyrockets as she imagines what they must think of her. Her thinking errors are: *They think I'm weird and annoying* and *They don't want me here.*

One of the seniors says, "Hey."

Steffie quickly mumbles something about studying for a Spanish quiz. Then she races off to the library, relieved to be out of that situation.

Problem solved? Nope. In fact, Steffie's response made her problem worse. Yes, she felt immediate relief to escape the kids who, according to her thinking errors, didn't want her around. But running away just made her fear of them stronger. Next time she sees them, she'll be more anxious, not less. This is why relying on avoidance and safety behaviors is problematic.

Relief from anxiety is a strong reward to your brain. It's kind of like when you give a dog a treat to get it to perform a trick. The dog can't think of anything except how to get that reward. Similarly, Steffie's brain so badly wants the relief it gets by running to the library that it will keep pressing her to run, even if her anxiety gets stronger as a result.

Another way avoidance and safety behaviors strengthen anxiety is by not giving you a chance to learn something new. What if the senior who said "hey" was about to compliment Steffie on her cool sweatshirt? Going to the library kept Steffie from learning that.

Avoidance and safety behaviors also keep you from learning that you can tolerate some anxiety. Suppose Steffie had stayed in the gym hallway and the seniors left her alone. She might have learned that her thinking error, *They don't want me here,* only caused a low level of anxiety. She might have discovered that she was actually okay with that low level. As a result, her belief in her thinking error would have diminished.

As long as you believe in your thinking errors, they will have power over you. If you can give up your belief in your thinking errors—whatever they are—you can decrease your anxiety. You may even eliminate them entirely. In a nutshell, by reducing your belief in your thinking errors, CBT gives you relief from social anxiety. In this sense, knowledge is power!

EXPOSURES ALLOW YOUR BRAIN TO REWIRE

Of course, it would be great if you could just will your beliefs to change. I'm quite certain you've tried at some point to reason with yourself about the truth of your beliefs. Or if you haven't, your parents, friends, teachers, or others have tried to help you see reason. But anxiety is not usually reasonable, and it doesn't get better by willing yourself to think more rationally.

The quickest and most effective way to change your beliefs is by changing your behavior. You may have tried this on your own. Perhaps you willed yourself to say hi to that guy you think is cute. But then you couldn't bring yourself to do it because your anxiety kicked in. That's probably because you didn't have an effective way to face your anxiety. The CBT program in this book fixes that by walking you through the process of doing *exposures*. The basic technique of exposures is to gradually face a situation that triggers your anxiety, while at the same time not engaging in any avoidance or safety behaviors. Exposures give your brain the opportunity to *rewire*, to learn different beliefs and behaviors.

In the CBT Social Anxiety Relief Program, you will conduct exposure experiments that allow you to gain information that contradicts your fear-based beliefs. In fact, research has shown that exposures are the most effective technique to alleviate anxiety. Millions of individuals of all ages have used CBT to conquer their anxiety by gradually facing their fears. Doing exposures allows your brain to learn to be less afraid and less anxious. Exposures allow you to see that what you fear most will happen doesn't actually happen.

In sum, changing your *behaviors* (by facing feared situations, without doing the behaviors you have relied on to cope with your social anxiety) changes your *cognitions* (thoughts). This, in a nutshell, describes the process of cognitive behavioral therapy.

I know this may still sound scary. Many teens tell me this. I'm asking you to trust me—and the science behind CBT—to guide you. In this book, you will learn how to use CBT to conquer your social anxiety. You will be able to decide at every step of the way how fast you want to go and how much you want to challenge yourself. You will have the knowledge and tools of CBT guiding you, making your efforts manageable and successful. You will learn to use what the world's most effective clinicians use to help millions find relief from anxiety.

THE FIVE STEPS OF YOUR CBT SOCIAL ANXIETY RELIEF PROGRAM

Your CBT program has five steps you will do in sequential order. As you continue to work the program, you'll keep cycling through these steps, each time with a new situation. The steps are:

1. Create a trigger situations list.

2. Identify avoidance and safety behaviors.

3. Build an exposure ladder.

4. Run an exposure experiment.

5. Climb more rungs on the ladder.

Let's see how this whole process flows with a real-life example. After a brief overview of each step, you'll read Steffie's report to see what she did in that step. In the chapters that follow, I'll explain how you can do each step yourself.

Don't worry if you don't get all the details now. The point here is to get a feel for the overall process. Before you agree to do this CBT program, I want you to know what you're agreeing to!

Step 1. Create a trigger situations list.

First, you will pay attention to, or monitor, the situations in which you feel anxious about being judged negatively by others. These are called *trigger situations* because they trigger feelings of anxiety, fear, or discomfort. In Step 1, you will make a list of the situations that trigger you.

Steffie's Report

I thought about all the social situations that make me anxious, from when I leave home to when I go to bed. I wrote in my diary about all the situations each day of the week that make me uncomfortable. The main ones are parties and talking to kids I don't know. Both of these freak me out! Parties are the worst. Luckily, parties don't happen often. But I'm supposed to talk to kids I don't know many times every day.

Over the past few days, I monitored each situation that triggers my anxiety. I realized that there are more situations than I thought. For example, I've always avoided school basketball and football games. I would convince myself that I didn't like those events and that I should study instead. I also identified other situations that make me uncomfortable. For example, walking through the main entrance at school when all of the popular kids are hanging out is super awkward. I decided to add those events to my trigger situations list. Here's my list:

- Parties
- Entering the campus main gate
- Walking around campus
- Talking to kids I don't know well
- Standing in line at the cafeteria
- Lunchtime
- Dances
- Sports events

Step 2: Identify avoidance and safety behaviors.

As we discussed in chapter 1, *avoidance behaviors* refer to what you actively do to avoid being in a trigger situation. This includes escaping from a situation after you realize it is a trigger situation for you. *Safety behaviors* are things you say or do to make it less likely you will feel the anxiety you expect will happen in a particular trigger situation. In Step 2, you will identify the avoidance and safety behaviors you use in each of your trigger situations.

Steffie's Report

In step 2, I figured out how I deal with my anxiety in each of my eight trigger situations. I looked at all the examples of avoidance and safety behaviors listed in this book and realized I do a lot of them.

When I thought about the trigger situation of entering through the campus main gate, I realized I get stressed because lots of kids hang out there, especially the popular kids. When I get there, I check the size of the crowd. If it's too big, I walk around to the side entrance. Or I put in my earbuds and rush through the main gate, like I'm late, even if I'm not.

For the trigger situation of walking around campus, I try to find my close friends. Usually I text to see where they'll be, but often they're too busy to text back. So, I text again if I don't see them where we usually hang. If I still don't hear from them, I go to my locker, even if I don't need to, just to act like I'm doing something.

I wrote down these behaviors for my first two trigger situations. So far, my list of avoidance and safety behaviors looks like this:

Entering the campus main gate
- Enter by another entrance
- Use earbuds
- Check crowd size
- Rush

Walking around campus
- Rely on BFFs for safety
- Text BFFs for certainty of whereabouts
- Avoid unsafe places
- Act like I'm busy

Step 3. Build an exposure ladder.

After you have created your trigger situations list and know your avoidance and safety behaviors, you will rate the level of fear you feel in each situation when refraining from doing any avoidance and safety behaviors. You'll use a scale called SUDS—which is described in the next chapter—to make your ratings.

To create an exposure ladder, you'll rank all your trigger situations according to the level of fear you feel in each, from lowest (at the bottom) to highest (at the top). Creating an exposure ladder gives you a general plan you can follow to gradually face the situations that trigger you.

Here is Steffie's exposure ladder for entering the campus main gate.

4. Rush (SUDS 6)

3. Enter by another entrance (SUDS 5)

2. Use earbuds (SUDS 5)

1. Check crowd (SUDS 4)

Step 4. Run an exposure experiment.

You'll run exposures much like you run a science experiment. You'll make a prediction about the outcome and rate how much you believe your prediction. You'll also rate your anxiety level before and after the exposure.

In most cases, you'll start with the trigger situation lowest on your exposure ladder—the one least fearful for you. You will identify the avoidance and safety behaviors you are willing to eliminate in that situation. You will keep doing exposures until you have successfully completed all the rungs on your ladder and given up all your avoidance and safety behaviors. Think of exposures as practice: you need to practice doing something different before you feel comfortable with it.

Steffie's Report

I made a commitment to myself to work on my first exposure ladder, starting with the bottom rung, which was entering the main gate without checking the crowd.

When I got to school, I put in my earbuds. I could do that because using earbuds is the safety behavior for the next rung on my ladder. As I went through the main gate, I focused on my music. I kind of rushed a bit but I didn't check how many kids were there. I was surprised I didn't feel tempted to use a side entrance. The exposure was easier than I thought!

After I did it, I wrote down my anxiety rating. It was only a SUDS rating of 3. That was lower than I thought it would be (which was a 4). I had also said beforehand that I believed 100 percent in my prediction that I'd sweat and get panicky if I went through the main gate. But that didn't happen. After my first exposure, my belief in that prediction went down to 50 percent. I had actual data that showed me things were changing. And for the better!

I decided to repeat this rung in case my first try was a fluke. Turned out it wasn't, and by the end of the week I was ready for the next rung. That rung was also easier than I expected.

I did run into a setback at the top rung. I guess it's hard for me not to rush. One morning, I got stuck in a crowd at the gate and tried to rush through. That wasn't working, so I panicked and ran to a side entrance. The next day, I went back down a rung and did some easier exposures before I was ready to try the hardest one again. When I finally did, I was able to walk through the main gate without doing any avoidance or safety behaviors. The most amazing thing was that I could do it day after day, feeling no more than minor anxiety.

Step 5. Climb more rungs on the ladder.

After you complete enough exposures to feel comfortable on a given rung of your exposure ladder, you will move up to the next rung. After you complete all the rungs on that ladder, you will pick a trigger situation to tackle next and create a ladder for it.

Steffie's Report

After I completed my first exposure, I reached step 5: climb more rungs. I completed those rungs. Then I went back to my list of trigger situations so I could start another ladder. I saw that walking around campus by myself was the next hardest. I thought it might be easier now that I could walk through the main gate without doing any avoidance or safety behaviors. At this point, I was picking up confidence and eager to keep climbing more ladders!

FAQS

Have a question? That's common after learning about the five steps of the CBT Social Anxiety Relief Program. Here are the most common questions I get from teens, plus answers.

Q: *This process seems really hard. What if I'm not sure I can do it?*

A: The CBT program can be challenging, for sure. However, I've found that most teens with social anxiety can and do succeed with it. Remember, this book will guide you, step by step, so you won't have to figure it out on your own.

This question is about what we call *anticipatory anxiety*. That means that when you think about a future situation in which you expect to feel uncomfortable, you feel anxious. Just thinking about the situation—anticipating it—is enough to make you anxious.

Unfortunately, anticipatory anxiety can cause you to avoid a situation altogether or do other avoidance and safety behaviors that keep you trapped in an anxiety cycle. You're anxious about a situation, so you avoid it. That makes you more anxious. And your increased anxiety makes you more determined to avoid the situation. And around you go!

It's important to know that anticipatory anxiety is normal. In fact, it's to be expected. It's equally important to keep in mind that being anxious about the CBT program doesn't mean you won't be able to succeed at it. Nor does it mean that you're taking on more than you can handle.

Initially, if you're focused on what scares you, you may miss all your small victories. If this is happening, I suggest taking five minutes before you go to bed and recalling three times you were in a trigger situation and felt okay. You can write these down in your notebook or phone. Look over your list of victories whenever you start to feel the process is getting hard.

Q: *How long will the process take?*

A: The short answer is that the more exposures you do, the faster you will start to feel better.

That said, the time it takes will be different for each person. If you're motivated and disciplined, you might start to feel some relief almost immediately. If you have avoided many social situations throughout your life, the process may take longer; you may have more exposure ladders to climb.

Since you'll be working at your own pace, how long it takes to complete each exposure ladder will also vary. The more often a trigger situation happens (or that you can make happen), the more chances you'll have to do exposures and build success. For example, if your trigger situation is walking between classes, you might be able to do an exposure six times a day. But if your trigger situation is going to a party, that probably won't be possible even once a week. Picking frequent situations will help to move the process along more quickly. If that sounds too challenging, don't worry; I'll show you how break down frequent situations so you feel confident tackling them.

Q: *I'm not really like Steffie. What if I don't relate to the examples I've read so far?*

A: As we saw in chapter 1, social anxiety has many faces. Not all the examples can cover all the many faces. Perhaps, for you, social anxiety is worrying about having sweaty palms or about using your computer in front of others. Or perhaps it's about not getting any likes on a social media post.

On the surface, each of these faces of anxiety seems different. Yet they all have a common core fear: that you will be negatively evaluated by others. The chapters that follow feature many different presentations of social anxiety, along with ideas for exposures to address them. With a little creativity, you'll be able to plan exposures that target your specific fears.

CHAPTER 3

Your CBT Toolbox

Before you start the first step of your CBT Social Anxiety Relief Program, I want to introduce you to some tools you'll be using. Come back to this chapter whenever you are working a step that calls for certain tools. In this toolbox you'll find the Subjective Units of Discomfort Scale, or SUDS; belief in prediction (BIP) ratings; and types of thinking errors.

SUDS: MEASURING ANXIETY

The goal of this CBT program is to lower your social anxiety so you are comfortable in situations that make you uncomfortable now. To do this successfully, you need to be able to measure your level of anxiety in different situations. The tool you'll use for this is the *Subjective Units of Discomfort Scale*, or *SUDS* for short. It works like a thermometer, with high and low ratings for relatively "cool" or "hot" anxiety.

You will use SUDS ratings frequently in this program. First, you'll use them to create your trigger situations list. The rating you give each situation will help you plan the order in which you do exposures, from easiest (lowest SUDS) to hardest (highest SUDS).

Second, you'll use SUDS ratings to measure your anxiety level as you progress through your exposures. Reductions in your SUDS ratings show you're getting more comfortable in trigger situations.

Assigning SUDS ratings can help you to feel a greater sense of control in situations that kick up strong emotions.

The Scale

Using the SUDS, you will rate your level of anxiety or discomfort on a scale of 0 to 10. The scale looks like this:

SUDS Rating	Your Feeling
0	Totally relaxed, no anxiety or discomfort at all
1	Very minimal anxiety or discomfort, alert and concentrating well
2	Minimal anxiety or discomfort
3	Mild anxiety or discomfort, no effect on daily functioning
4	Mild to moderate anxiety or discomfort
5	Moderate anxiety or discomfort, some effect on functioning
6	Moderate to strong anxiety or discomfort
7	Quite anxious or uncomfortable, strong effect on functioning
8	Very anxious or uncomfortable, can't concentrate
9	Extremely anxious or highly uncomfortable
10	Worst anxiety I've ever felt

You might want to copy this scale in your notebook or take a photo of it with your phone so you can quickly access it throughout your CBT program.

I want to stress that SUDS ratings are subjective—that is, they represent your personal point of view. There are no right or wrong SUDS ratings.

What you consider "the worst anxiety imaginable" might look completely different than what someone else considers the worst anxiety imaginable. Similarly, what feels like mild anxiety to you might not feel mild to someone else.

For example, in the situation of speaking in class, one person's SUDS rating may be a 10, while another's may be a 4. These differences don't matter. They're to be expected. What is important is that you personally know what each SUDS rating means to you. That way you can be consistent in your ratings. To help you get acquainted with the scale, try the following exercise.

Exercise: My SUDS Ratings

Take a few moments to go through each of the ratings. Start with 0 and work your way up the scale to 10. Clarify what each rating means to you by asking yourself:

- When do I feel (or have felt) a SUDS of 0?

- How would I describe my anxiety at a SUDS of 0?

Feel free to make notes beside the scale. Remember, this is your personal scale. Repeat these questions for each level (1, 2, 3, etc.). You may feel some anxiety doing this exercise, especially when you get to the higher ratings. This is because you are indirectly exposing yourself to the situations in which you feel those ratings. This is a good thing! It means you're already on your way to conquering your social anxiety.

If you find that doing this exercise triggers you, repeat it over and over until your level of discomfort decreases. It doesn't matter how many times you need to repeat this exercise; I promise your discomfort will decrease if you stick with it.

MEASURING YOUR BELIEF IN PREDICTIONS

As we discussed in chapter 2, thinking errors play a big part in fueling social anxiety. What you think (and fully believe) will happen determines how you handle trigger situations.

For example, Steffie thinks she'll be embarrassed if she goes to a party. Therefore, she avoids going to parties. If we ask her to predict what will happen at a party, she'll predict getting embarrassed. If we ask her to rate how much she believes in that prediction, she might say 100 percent. She's certain she'll be embarrassed!

In the CBT program, you will make predictions about what you think will happen when you run an exposure experiment. You will assign a percentage to your belief that a predicted outcome will occur. That percentage is your *belief in prediction (BIP) rating*.

For example, you might predict that if you go to swim practice (a trigger situation), kids will laugh at your hair when it gets wet. If you feel certain that that reaction (predicted outcome) will happen, you will give it a BIP rating of 100 percent.

Why is doing this helpful? Because it gives you a basis to compare. After you run an exposure experiment, you will check if your prediction came true. For example, perhaps you discover that the kids didn't laugh at your wet hair. Still, even if they didn't do it that time, you worry they might do it another time. So you might lower your BIP rating to 50 percent. After some more exposures, your rating might get lower—say to 10 percent. In this way, your BIP ratings help you monitor your progress.

Exercise: My BIP Ratings

Like with SUDS ratings, it's helpful to get a bit of practice ahead of time.

Think of something that is a trigger situation for you. Now consider what outcome you'd expect if you refrain from doing any avoidance or safety behaviors in that situation. Ask yourself, *How strongly do I believe in my prediction?* Assign a percentage (from 0 to 100 percent) to your belief.

TYPES OF THINKING ERRORS

During the CBT process, you won't be asked to identify the types of thinking errors you have. However, knowing as much as you can about your thinking errors will make it easier to identify your avoidance and safety behaviors (which are based on your thinking errors). So let's look more closely at them now.

Four types of thinking errors are most common in social anxiety: *mind reading, futurizing, catastrophizing,* and *overprobablizing.* You may have one or all of these types. They may also overlap at times.

Mind Reading

Mind reading occurs when you believe you can tell what other people are thinking. You might even believe you are uniquely skilled at judging how others feel about you. Of course, we'd all love to have a mind-reading superpower. Then we wouldn't have to worry about whether others like us, and we could surround ourselves with others who think we're attractive, cool, fun, and the best.

However, the truth is there's no way to really know what someone else thinks about us—short of asking them. Doing that is especially hard if you have social anxiety, because the last thing you want to do is walk up to someone and ask, "What do you think of me?" And I'm not suggesting you do that. Even if you did give it a try, you'd have no way to know if the other person was being truthful. Rather, what's important for the CBT program is that you become aware of when and why and how you engage in mind reading.

One characteristic of mind reading is that it tends to focus on negatives. Not only are you convinced you know what others think about you, you're *sure* they're thinking negative things and judging you in the worst possible way. Here are some examples of mind reading:

Barb thinks I'm stupid.

Jose thinks I'm weird.

They won't talk to me because they think I'll be annoying if I join the conversation.

Kids will think my social media post is boring.

Asha doesn't like it when I smile at her.

They don't want me around.

Futurizing

Futurizing (also sometimes called *fortune telling*) occurs when your mind focuses on the future rather than on the present. Of course, there are plenty of good reasons to think about the future. And if you didn't think about the future, you couldn't make plans or set goals or work toward any form of improvement. However, futurizing in this book is about thinking errors in which you wrongly predict what will happen in a given situation.

As with mind reading, futurizing tends to emphasize negatives. For example, you believe you'll get so anxious giving your oral report next week that your mind will go blank, you won't be able to say a word, everyone will laugh at you, and then they'll talk about you behind your back. Your futurizing prepares you for a distressing outcome. You already feel terrified, even though nothing has happened yet. You forget that no one can accurately predict the future. When you futurize, you block your brain from considering more likely outcomes that aren't so negative, such as, "I may get nervous when I give that oral report, but I'll probably be able to get through it."

It's as if your mind is telling you the way to stop bad things from happening is to continually think about them happening. In fact, this is why people futurize. They hold the mistaken belief that they can somehow prevent negative things from happening.

Here are some examples of futurizing:

If I raise my hand in class, I'll stutter and people will laugh at me.

If I go to the dance and ask Maria to dance, she'll say no.

If I tell Tom I don't like punk music, he'll tell everyone I have poor taste.

If I say hi to Jackson, he won't say hi back.

If I put on a bathing suit, everyone will make fun of my skinny legs.

Catastrophizing

Catastrophizing involves imagining the worst-case scenario as the only possible explanation or outcome. When you are in a trigger situation, your mind tends to immediately go to the worst possible case. It speeds past any alternative explanations or outcomes and settles on the worst.

You might think this is helpful because it keeps you prepared. You can't be caught off guard if you've already thought of the worst possible outcome, right? Not exactly. Because when you believe that a negative outcome is a forgone conclusion, you are left paralyzed by anxiety. Even if the catastrophe you anticipated doesn't materialize, you expect it will happen the next time.

Here are some examples of catastrophizing:

I will fall off the balance beam and twist my ankle, and no one will even help me up.

I will botch the experiment. When we get an F, my lab partner will blame me.

Not a single person will talk to me at the party.

Sarah didn't text me today. She doesn't want to be friends anymore.

I'll be so nervous that I'll throw up at dinner, and Marco will never ask me out again.

Overprobablizing

Overprobablizing builds on catastrophizing in that it means assuming the worst-case scenario will occur every single time you are in a trigger situation. It means you overestimate or exaggerate the likelihood something bad will occur; in your mind, it is going to happen for certain. You aren't comforted at all by the fact that the objective odds of it happening are low. For example, experts have calculated the odds of an airplane going down to be as low as 1 in 11 million. Yet, if you fear flying, when you get on the plane, it may feel to you like a 90 percent chance.

When it comes to social anxiety, overprobablizing works in a similar manner. You may have successfully given an oral report many times since you got to high school. Yet, the minute you're called on to give one now, you can only think of the worst-case scenario: you'll freeze, the class will laugh at you, you'll get a failing grade. You forget all the times you managed to do it okay *and* earned a good grade. Let's say that out of ten reports you've given, only one didn't go well. Although, based on past experience, you have a 90 percent chance of success, overprobablizing tells you this upcoming report will 100 percent be a disaster.

One problematic effect of overprobablizing is that it can make you so anxious that you do mess up, even when objectively speaking you have every reason to succeed. Here are some examples of overprobablizing:

If I take another skating lesson, I'll be as awkward as last time. I'll be the worst skater there.

If I post a selfie, I'll never get a single like.

No one else will wear a short dress to the prom. I'll be humiliated if I wear one.

Everyone who hears me sing says I'm off-key. I won't sing in front of anyone.

If I walk in the school hallway alone, not one kid will say hi.

FAQS

Q: *I'm confused about these tools. How will I know when to use them?*

A: In the chapters that follow, whenever you're directed to use one of these tools, you can refer back to this chapter and refresh your memory. You don't need to memorize them all now! The more you use each tool, the easier it will become. These tools will be useful for many years to come, as they can help you continue to manage social anxiety for a lifetime.

Q: *What if all my anxiety ratings are over a 10?*

A: Many teens feel as if their anxiety is so high that it merits more than a 10. You might feel, for example, that kissing your crush would be a 20. Or even a 95! Even if you feel that way, what is important is that you anchor your rating of a 10 at the most anxious you've ever felt. Therefore, you can't (and no one can) have a SUDS rating higher than a 10. Remember, it's just like the pain scale your doctor may have used if you broke a bone or had an ailment that led to pain.

Wanting to use SUDS ratings higher than 10 can mean several things. For instance, you might think your distress is higher than a 10 because you're worried you can't handle this CBT program. In other words, you're futurizing, catastrophizing, and overprobablizing before you even get started.

Wanting to use more than 10 can also be avoidance. You might be used to avoiding a trigger situation, so you tell yourself a superhigh SUDS rating will give you a reason to keep avoiding it. In both cases, all I ask is that you give it a try: stick to 1 to 10 for ratings and see how the program works for you.

Finally, the desire to make superhigh SUDS ratings could mean that your social anxiety is so severe you can't succeed at the CBT program without extra support. This rarely happens, but some teens need the support of a CBT clinician and possibly medication. I suggest you consider talking to a professional with expertise in cognitive behavioral therapy if you continue to struggle with SUDS ratings.

CHAPTER 4

Creating a Trigger Situations List

Now you're ready to take the first step in the CBT Social Anxiety Relief Program. Congratulations in advance! This step involves coming up with a complete list of trigger situations—that is, all the situations in which social anxiety arises for you.

In chapter 1, you met Martin, the senior who gets anxious speaking in class and who's considering an online college due to his social anxiety. Like most teens, he has a superbusy schedule with homework, special projects, and all that's involved in applying for college. But also, like many teens with social anxiety, he's most comfortable when he feels he has some control over his life. The CBT program offers a way for Martin to get more of a handle on his anxiety, and that makes the time and effort it will require worth it to him. Martin will be doing this first step along with you.

In this chapter, you will do three things. First, you will monitor yourself and identify trigger situations that occur for you throughout the week. Second, you will come up with a list of these situations. Finally, you will use the SUDS to rate these situations. So let's get started!

MONITOR YOUR TRIGGER SITUATIONS

For this task, please put on your researcher hat. As a researcher, you're going to study your daily habits. You're going to track how you react in different situations. It might be tempting to rely on your gut response to choose the trigger situations for your list. However, I've noticed it's easy to leave out important situations when one jumps too quickly to make a list. So, putting on your researcher hat will help you slow down and result in the most accurate and useful list.

The best way to create an accurate trigger situations list is to mentally—and slowly—walk yourself through a typical day and review all the situations you usually run into. You don't need to do this in real time, adding to your list throughout the day—although you could do that if you want. Rather, sit down at the end of the day and carefully recall trigger situations from the moment you woke up. You'll also want to think about trigger situations that may not happen often but that you face from time to time. These might include vacations, weekend activities, family gatherings, going to restaurants, and so on.

Find a nice research corner for yourself and walk through the day in your mind. Your research corner could be a comfy nest of pillows or the kitchen table or a picnic bench. It could be any spot where you can sit quietly and study your behaviors. The important thing at this step of the process is to go over your day in great detail. You want to catch those situations that might otherwise slip under the radar. Be sure to include situations that you currently avoid because they trigger you.

Your Daily Monitoring Diary

To notice situations you might be avoiding, review your weekday by day. Review each day hour by hour. You will use the Daily Monitoring Diary to do this. It includes separate pages for each day, so you'll have enough room to write down your notes. You can download the Daily Monitoring Diary from this book's website at http://www.newharbinger.com/47056 and print it out. Or if you prefer, create a diary in your notebook or even on your phone.

Here's how Martin filled out his Daily Monitoring Diary and monitored his trigger situations.

Martin's Daily Monitoring Diary

	Monday
7–9 a.m.	Freaked about English / old jean shirt is in the wash, have to wear red flannel
9–10 a.m.	Super anxious walking by student lounge on the way to Chem
10–11 a.m.	Chemistry: Joe was late and I was afraid I'd get another partner for lab
11 a.m.–12 p.m.	Joe got there in time for lab, phew
12–1 p.m.	Lunch: skipped lunch cause I didn't want to see anyone / went straight to library
1–2 p.m.	Study hall: spent most of time worrying about English
2–3 p.m.	AP English: had to read out loud
3–4 p.m.	Felt nauseated after Eng, went home
4–5 p.m.	
5–6 p.m.	
6–7 p.m.	Still kind of nauseated, asked Mom to make me soup for dinner
7–8 p.m.	Told Dad I couldn't go with him to pick up pizza
8–9 p.m.	Stayed in my room cause my sister's BFF was over watching TV
9–10 p.m.	
10 p.m.–12 a.m.	

Martin's Report

I sat down Monday evening to review my day and fill out the monitoring sheet. I realized I start to feel anxious even before I get to school. I know I'll be in situations that make me anxious, I just don't know what all of them are yet. In a way, it's worse than if I knew exactly what to expect. I always have to be on alert.

If it's a day for World Politics or AP English, I feel anxious the minute I wake up. I put on low-key clothes and wear drab colors so I can blend in. So I filled in the 7 to 9 a.m. slots for all five weekdays. Then I filled in the hours I have World Politics or AP English.

World Politics makes me anxious because it's a discussion class. Mrs. Chu always calls on me because she wants me to increase my participation grade, which is poor. If I have to give an oral presentation, I freak out for days. Sometimes I tell my parents I'm sick. The best is when I can do the oral report just for Mrs. Chu. But I never know if she'll let me.

Lots of times in AP English we read aloud. Right now we're reading Shakespeare. It's impossible to read out loud because it's not normal English, and I sound like an idiot reading it. Mr. Riordan says everyone feels awkward reading this stuff. I skip class whenever I know it's going to be my turn to read. If I haven't said anything in class for a while, I can be pretty sure Mr. Riordan will call on me.

On days when I have other classes—Chemistry, Math, and Spanish—I feel relieved. Those classes are easy and don't require much class participation. In general, everyone in Chem and Math keeps to themselves and does their work. I can do Spanish at home.

Morning recess makes me feel uncomfortable. I go to my locker and hope I don't run into anyone who wants to talk to me. Walking between classes is also hard. Walking past the student lounge is the worst. I never go in there. I tell myself I don't have any reason to. But as I was doing my monitoring diary, I realized that's a rationalization. If I have to give someone a book, it would be easier to go into the lounge instead of just hoping to run into them. So I added the lounge to my monitoring sheet, even though it's a situation I avoid.

The minute school is over, I leave campus. I don't even go back to my locker because kids are there. I don't feel comfortable making chitchat. I wanted to join the Robotics Club afterschool because I like that stuff and it would look good for colleges. But I got so worried about going to the first meeting that I bailed on it.

On weekends, I stay home and do homework or play video games with kids in different cities. If my parents make me go out to dinner with them, I try to avoid anyone I know from school or any kids my age.

I monitored myself for a few more days. Then I made adjustments to my Diary. On Friday, when my dad made me go to the grocery store with him, I ran into a kid from Math class. I realized I had to add that trigger situation. I was surprised how many slots were filled in. Almost all day long, I'm worried I'll be in a trigger situation. Even if I think I have a way to avoid things like chitchat, there are a million times a day some kid might try to chat me up. It makes me feel exhausted and like I don't want to go to school!

Tips for Daily Monitoring

Fill out as many time slots as you can. Fill out the form for each day of the week. If the same situation occurs on multiple days, list them again. The idea is to get a full picture of how often and when a trigger happens. You won't need to reference specific time slots during the rest of the CBT process.

Don't rush it! The most helpful way to make sure your trigger situations list is complete is to monitor yourself for a few days. Add any new trigger situations that you observe or that you remember. A situation doesn't have to occur every day to be on your list.

Don't talk yourself down. As you make your list, be careful not to confuse anxiety and preference. Just because you're anxious in a situation doesn't mean you don't like that situation or don't want it in your life. Martin *rationalized* not going into the student lounge. When you rationalize avoidance, you try to convince yourself you don't want to participate in situations that trigger social anxiety, even if you really do.

For example, suppose working out at the gym makes you anxious. Instead of thinking, *I want to go to the gym, but going to the gym makes me anxious*, you rationalize, *I don't like working out*. Or suppose studying with others makes you anxious. Instead of thinking, *I'd like to join that study group, but it makes me anxious*, you rationalize, *I study better when I'm by myself*. In these ways, you convince yourself your avoidance isn't really a problem.

Don't leave trigger situations like these off your list because you think you don't like them. If anything, these are the situations you want to work on so you can participate in them without feeling anxious.

Keep in mind common triggers. As you complete your Daily Monitoring Diary, use the following list to help jog your memory. Make sure that you aren't overlooking situations that trigger you. However, if you miss a trigger situation or two, you can easily add them later. Here are examples of trigger situations common to teens with social anxiety:

- Giving an oral presentation in class
- Raising your hand in class
- Answering a question in front of others
- Performing or speaking in front of others at an assembly
- Performing in front of others in music practice
- Performing in front of others at sports practice or competition
- Joining a group of peers who are already talking
- Making small talk with someone you don't know well
- School recess
- Lunchtime
- Moving between classes
- A party or dance
- A sporting event
- Being watched while writing
- Being watched while on the computer or the phone
- Being watched while eating
- Meeting someone new

- Using the restroom in the presence of others
- Interacting with teachers or persons in authority positions
- Inviting someone to do something
- Being the center of attention (intentionally or by accident)
- Making a special request, such as returning an item to a store or asking for a favor
- Stating your opinion
- Posting on social media
- Sharing transportation with someone you don't know well, such as by bus or carpool

COMPILE YOUR TRIGGER SITUATIONS LIST

The next part of this task is quite straightforward. You're going to take all the trigger situations for the different days in your Daily Monitoring Dairy and compile them in a single list. Although it's a straightforward exercise, you will have to think about how best to list each situation. And you'll want to break some general situations into smaller sub-situations or possibly group some situations together.

Here's how Martin described compiling his trigger situations list.

Martin's Report

My list ended up with about twenty trigger situations. There were so many, I felt kind of like I might not be able to do this! But I kept going.

It got better when I realized most of the things I wrote in my early-morning time slot could be combined into one trigger situation. Anxiety about getting out of bed, worry about being called on in World Politics, worry about a pop quiz in Spanish—all those are my anxieties about what will happen at school. I found out from monitoring that I don't feel triggered much on weekends. Then I'm only triggered if something like going out to dinner or the movies happens.

I did create a sub-situation for early mornings: getting dressed for school. Lots of my early-morning worries are about messing up in class and kids noticing I'm nervous. But I also worry about how I look to other kids. My SUDS rating for getting dressed is only a 3, compared with 4 to 5 for the other early-morning triggers. I think that's because I can choose what I wear.

I also got a little confused figuring out my classroom trigger situations. I realized that giving an oral report is hands down the most triggering. So I decided to make that a sub-situation. Giving an oral report is for sure a 10 on the SUDS, no matter which class it is. So I grouped all oral reports into one sub-situation.

I know my most triggering classes are World Politics and AP English. I thought about combining them as one trigger situation. But my SUDS ratings for them are different, so I kept them separate. Mr. Riordan's English class changes a lot, because he has us do more different kinds of things. Like some days we have quiet writing periods, which are much less triggering. So, it really varies, which makes it super stressful until I know what we are doing on a given day.

I did a lot of thinking about the trigger situations that occur between classes. On my monitoring sheet, these are listed every day, several times a day. I decided to make morning recess its own situation. Then I combined all the trigger situations that involve walking between classes. Really, what I feel walking between Math and English isn't that different from what I feel walking between English and Art. It just involves a greater distance.

What is different, though, is any time I have to go past the student lounge. So I made that its own trigger situation. It has a higher SUDS rating than just walking between classes. And I included going into the lounge, which I always avoid doing.

Tips for Compiling Your Trigger List

List each situation only once. Even if you listed "taking the bus to school" as a trigger situation five times during the week, you will only list it once on your trigger situations list.

Consider breaking situations into more specific sub-situations. Pay close attention to what specifically triggers you in each situation. For example, suppose "attending Math class" is one of your trigger situations. But you also can pinpoint that "raising my hand in Math" is something that especially triggers you in this class. Now you have a choice: You may decide to include both "attending Math class" and "raising my hand in Math" on your trigger situations list. Or you may decide that raising your hand in this class is really the thing that triggers you and the reason you listed Math on your monitoring sheet. In that case, you will put only "raising my hand in Math" on your trigger situations list. Martin described how he created sub-situations for getting dressed for school and for giving an oral report.

Consider your fear level. Even though the next task will be to complete your SUDS ratings, you might want to consider your anxiety level now, as you compile your list. For example, Martin made World Politics and AP English separate trigger situations because they had different SUDS ratings. As you get more familiar with this process, you'll feel more comfortable moving between the different tasks.

Look for overlap in your trigger situations. Suppose your list includes both "walk from class to class" and "walk from class to lunch." Is there unnecessary overlap, or is there an important difference? If the trigger in both situations is having to say hi or having people look at you, then you can combine them. However, maybe walking from class to lunch involves much longer contact. Maybe you feel you have to explain why you can't go with other kids to the lunchroom. In that case, leave these as two separate trigger situations.

Remember, this is a work in progress! Don't worry if you aren't sure how to list some situations or if you feel as if your list is incomplete. You'll have a chance to revisit your list after you get some experience under your belt. In later chapters, you can refresh your list with whatever are your most currently pressing trigger situations.

RATE YOUR TRIGGER SITUATIONS

Now that you have your trigger situations list, it's time to put your research hat on again and do some measurements. This is when you use the SUDS tool. The goal is to know more specifically how you feel in each of these situations so you can (in later chapters) plan and execute exposure experiments.

Here is Martin's trigger situations list with his SUDS ratings, plus his comments about the ratings.

Martin's Report

After I compiled my list, I wrote down my SUDS ratings. In some cases, I already knew what the rating would be. Like I knew getting dressed for school is never more than a 3. I pictured myself in each situation and used the scale I had copied from chapter 3 to make my SUDS rating.

I ended up with a total of five 10s. Although chitchatting isn't always a 10, I don't have any ratings less than 3. That surprised me. I thought I'd have some 1s or 2s. But if I'm completely honest about it, my anxiety doesn't go below a 3 in any of these situations. I guess if I could come out of this CBT program with some 1 or 2 SUDS ratings, that would be pretty cool!

Trigger Situation	SUDS Rating
Wake up on school day and think about which classes I have	4-5
World Politics	7-8
AP English	6-9
Oral reports	10
Dress for school	3
Morning recess	4
Walk between classes	3-5
Walk past student lounge	6
Go into student lounge	10
Afterschool club	10
Post on social media	10
Chitchat in person	8-10
Go to a restaurant	8
Go to the store	8

Tips for Rating Your Trigger Situations

Refer to chapter 3. All the basic information you need for using SUDS is presented in chapter 3. Be sure to reread that section before you do your ratings. And refer back to it as often as you need to.

Use your gut. Rate your triggers relatively quickly. You're rating your feelings, and you don't want to overthink that. Follow your gut.

Use a range, if you need to. Some of your situations may be more general than others or include more variation from day to day. Even some situations that seem narrow or specific may have surprising amounts of variation. For example, suppose your trigger situation is speaking in class. However, when you think about it, you realize that speaking in Ms. Wong's science lab isn't anywhere near as uncomfortable as speaking in Mr. Hilton's English class. This is because the lab has only a dozen kids, while there are almost thirty students in English. Therefore you might give a SUDS range of 5 to 7 to span the variation in these two situations.

Review your ratings. After you have made your ratings based on your gut feelings, review the numbers you have assigned. Did you skip any? If so, rate them now. Also notice if your ratings are very uniform. For example, you might have made them all 10 or close to 10. If this is the case (especially if your ratings are all equal), see if you can distinguish between them. This could involve breaking out some less-anxiety-producing sub-situations. The idea is to end up with a list that includes both very uncomfortable (high SUDS) and less uncomfortable (low SUDS) trigger situations.

FAQS

Q: *What happens if I have too many trigger situations?*

A: There is no such thing as having too many trigger situations. You may feel a little overwhelmed or even discouraged if you have a lot of trigger situations, but having lots of triggers is normal!

You may be thinking, *I have so many triggers, how will I ever deal with all of them?* Try not to futurize. But do try to manage your thinking errors. Remember, as we discussed in chapter 3, you can't accurately predict the future. Take each step one at a time and assess as you go.

In fact, once you start doing exposures, you probably won't have to face every situation that's on your trigger list now. This is because of something we call *generalization*. What this means in simple terms is that what you do in one situation carries over into other situations. Generalization can work against you, but it can also work in your favor.

Here's how it can work against you, making you worry more. Suppose one of your trigger situations is standing in line at the school cafeteria. You may generalize that anxiety to similar situations, such as when you're in line at the grocery store. You might notice that you're uncomfortable in the grocery line even though you haven't felt anxiety there before. This is because your mind generalizes from one standing-in-line situation to other standing-in-line situations.

Fortunately, generalization can work the other way around as well. Let's say your SUDS rating for standing in line at the grocery store is lower than your SUDS rating for standing in line at the school cafeteria. So you decide to do exposures for standing in line at the grocery store first. And it works! Afterward, you feel less anxious standing in line there. But then you discover something unexpected. When you think about your SUDS rating for standing in line at the school cafeteria, it's lower! In fact, it's lower than your rating originally was for the store.

How can that be? The answer is generalization. Your brain learned it's not as bad, scary, or dangerous to stand in line at the grocery store as you predicted it would be. Your brain generalizes the learning from exposures at the grocery store to the related situation of standing in line at the cafeteria. This happens without fail to people of all ages who do CBT programs.

Q: *I kind of fudged it on keeping my monitoring diary. I mean, I already know what my trigger situations are without doing any monitoring. Is that a problem?*

A: That's a tough question to answer without knowing more about which situations you put on your list. Maybe you have an awesome memory. Even if you do, though, you can still miss some important situations. Leaving them off your list could end up making this program harder for you than it needs to be.

Let's say you got a bit impatient because you're so certain you already know your trigger situations. So you only list the situations that bother you most. This would probably result in a list with a narrow range of situations with pretty high SUDS ratings. When you start to do exposures, you won't have the benefit of being able to start with trigger situations that have lower SUDS ratings. You won't have the option to work on them baby step by baby step. This could make the CBT process much more difficult than it needs to be for you. It could even result in you not following through with an exposure plan, which would strengthen beliefs you have that you can't manage being in social situations comfortably.

Q: *I'm confused about the difference between trigger situations and sub-situations. Can you explain more about that?*

A: When I speak about a "trigger situation," I mean a general circumstance in which you feel anxiety and discomfort. However, many different things may be happening in that place or at that time. Some of those things may cause you more anxiety and others less.

Suppose you feel anxiety speaking in front of others at school. That's your general trigger situation. But now think about what else could be happening in situations that involve speaking in front of others. In English class, it might mean standing up and speaking to twenty kids about a book you didn't finish reading. Or during a hacker club meeting, it might mean telling half a dozen kids about computer code you wrote. Or, if you're in the drama club, it might mean reciting a speech on stage in front of hundreds. Your SUDS rating for each of these versions of the same basic trigger situation is likely to be very different.

This is where sub-situations come in. It might be helpful to break your general trigger situation of speaking in front of others into two or three sub-situations. You could do this based on how many people are present or on how well you know what you're speaking about. For instance, you might distinguish "speaking in front of my English class" from "speaking to kids in hacker club" and from "speaking on stage during a drama club performance." Identifying these specific situations will be helpful when you start designing exposures. You'll be able to start with easier situations and later move on to more difficult ones.

Q: *Will I have to do exposures for trigger situations that have a SUDS rating of 10? Because if I'm supposed to do that, I think I might quit now.*

A: This is a common worry teens have when they begin the CBT process. It is also, by the way, an example of catastrophizing and futurizing, as we discussed in chapter 3.

The answer is *no*, you won't have to do any exposures for which you have a 10 SUDS rating. At least, you won't while they are still a 10 for you. You'll only do exposures for those situations after you have given them a lower SUDS rating and feel ready to tackle them.

You might think, *That's impossible. No way am I lowering my SUDS rating for that 10!*

I know it might feel that way, but your brain is able to learn quickly from experience. If you're worried about having to face too many trigger situations or situations with a 10 SUDS rating, you can relax. The trigger situations list you compiled and the ratings you made in this first step of your CBT process won't stay the same. They will change a lot as you continue going through the steps. And that's the whole purpose of this process!

CHAPTER 5

Identifying Avoidance and Safety Behaviors

No one wants to feel pain or discomfort. And as you know, social anxiety can be painful and uncomfortable. It's natural to come up with strategies so you don't have to feel that way. Unfortunately, however, these strategies don't achieve their intended goal. Here are some examples.

Bella feels anxious when she has to use the school bathroom while others are present. She gets panicky when she thinks others can hear her urinate. Sometimes she is physically unable to pee. To avoid this painful situation, Bella has a strategy: she doesn't drink anything during the school day. But if she does have to go to the bathroom, she requests permission during class time to avoid anyone else being there. However, that's a last resort, because Bella is also embarrassed to leave during class.

Keto loves playing drums in the marching band at school. And he knows he's good at it. At football games, however, he gets uncomfortable. When all the popular jocks and cheerleaders are watching, he worries they'll think he is a nerd. He's especially uncomfortable when he has to wear a dorky uniform. Keto won't look anyone in the eye and tries to blend in as best he can. When athletes, cheerleaders, and others tell him what a great job he and the band are doing, he says things like, "Too bad we have to look like such idiots in these dumb hats and uniforms!" He takes off his uniform immediately and leaves the field as soon as his bandleader allows.

Amber is anxious interacting with people she doesn't consider close friends. As much as possible, she sticks with her best friend. She relies on that friend to act as a buffer and speak to other kids for her. When Amber has to walk alone between classes, she dashes out of class early so no one can talk to her.

Bella is focused on avoidance. Keto uses mainly safety behaviors. Amber uses both avoidance and safety behaviors. Each of the three relies on these behaviors to make it through daily life. But by doing so, they don't allow themselves the opportunity to overcome their anxiety. In order to overcome their social anxiety, they would have to identify and gradually stop using their avoidance and safety behaviors.

That's what you are going to work on in this chapter. You will investigate how you use avoidance and safety behaviors. First, we'll talk about the specifics of these behaviors and how teens typically use them, as well as why these behaviors are so problematic. Then you will go through all your trigger situations and identify the avoidance and safety behaviors you use in each.

AVOIDANCE BEHAVIORS

Avoiding situations that trigger discomfort is probably the most common way teens deal with social anxiety. However, everyone has different ways of avoiding. Some ways are more obvious than others. Building on the common avoidance behaviors listed in chapter 1, here's a more expanded list you can use as you get ready for the next step of the CBT process, in which you will identify your own avoidance behaviors:

- Not engage in eye contact
- Not raise your hand in class
- Not speak in class
- Not take a class that requires oral presentations
- Not use the camera in a virtual classroom
- Not attend a dance
- Leave an event early
- Not eat in front of others
- Not talk on the phone in front of others
- Not use the restroom in front of others
- Escape to the library
- Hide out in the restroom
- Stand outside of groups and not saying anything
- Spend time thinking of excuses for avoiding a situation
- Not share your opinions or preferences
- Imagine you're somewhere else and not really in the current situation

As you look over this list, you'll probably relate to some behaviors and others not so much. Some may appear to be similar to what you do yet not exactly the same. What they all have in common, though, is a strategy to avoid a triggering situation.

Most of the actions on the list are examples of *direct* avoidance behaviors. But some avoidance behaviors are considered *indirect*—that is, they only happen in your mind. You don't act out an actual behavior. The last behavior on the list ("imagine you're somewhere else and not really in the current situation") is indirect. Here's how it can work: Suppose you have lots of anxiety during school recess. When you see a mob of kids hanging out where you are, you imagine you're at an airport. You tell yourself all these kids are strangers. This strategy reduces your anxiety in the moment. We call that indirect avoidance because you're only doing it in your mind. You're not actually inside an airport. Indirect avoidance behaviors have the same undesirable effect as other types of avoidance behaviors, they just aren't as obvious to others.

SAFETY BEHAVIORS

In addition to avoidance, you might also engage in behaviors or mental actions to detect and prevent the outcomes you fear in trigger situations. As is the case with avoidance behaviors, you may find some safety behaviors listed here that you do, others that are similar, and some that you would never do. Take a look at this list and see what resonates:

- Pretend not to see others you don't know well
- Talk extra quietly
- Speak in short sentences
- Rehearse sentences in your mind before a social interaction
- Position yourself so others won't notice you (in an in-person or virtual classroom)
- Occupy yourself with your phone
- Wear earbuds

- Review in your mind what you said, how it sounded, what you believe others thought

- Try to keep tight control of your behavior

- Look closely at people and try to gauge their reactions to you

- Ask others about your performance or how they perceived your behavior

- Use alcohol or other drugs to help you feel more relaxed

- Hide your actions with your hand, your hair, a book, or an article of clothing

- Check for sweating or redness of your face in a mirror

- Spend a lot of time grooming prior to a social situation

Are some of these safety behaviors familiar? Again, this is a small sampling, and your own behaviors may be different. In addition, you may also find it a bit hard to tell whether some of the things you do are avoidance or safety behaviors. Don't worry about that. As you read on, you will find many examples of both types, including when they overlap. Most important, you don't have to be able to tell avoidance and safety behaviors apart in every situation in order to succeed at this program.

WHY AVOIDANCE AND SAFETY BEHAVIORS ARE PROBLEMATIC

By now, you probably have a good sense of why avoidance and safety behaviors are problematic. But let's spend a bit more time on this. Without getting too technical, I want to give you the information you need to truly understand why these behaviors, which seemingly help you cope, are actually feeding your anxiety. They're making it worse. This is true for both avoidance and safety behaviors.

Here are four reasons that show why any avoidance or safety behavior you do is troublesome:

Reason 1: It becomes a habit.

When you avoid doing something, you also avoid any negative outcome that might occur if you did that behavior. Your brain experiences temporary relief when the behavior stops or prevents anxiety. Over time, your brain learns that the behavior is effective and starts to rely on it more and more. Thus, a habit is formed. And once a habit is formed, it can be hard to break.

Psychologists call this *negative reinforcement*. It means that you avoid doing something so that a bad thing won't happen. For example, because Bella avoids using the school bathroom, she doesn't experience the negative outcome of getting panicky. Because avoidance keeps her from feeling panicky, she makes it a habit. After a while, she doesn't even think about doing anything different. She simply doesn't use the school bathroom, unless it's an extreme emergency.

Positive reinforcement works in the opposite way: you're rewarded for doing something well. For example, you get good grades and then go out for ice cream as a reward.

Your brain has a big role in the formation of habits. You see your avoidance and safety behaviors as life preservers or as safe havens. For example, you might stay close to your BFF so you won't feel the discomfort of being alone around other kids. Or you might continually check your phone for the same purpose. However, as these behaviors become a habit, your brain also associates them with danger.

Sound contradictory? Think for a minute about how this works. Suppose you look at your phone whenever you feel uncomfortable around people; you're using your phone as a life preserver. Or suppose the only place you'll eat at school is in the library; you see the library as your safe haven. Your phone and the library don't in themselves cause anxiety. But an anxious mind is tasked with keeping you out of danger. It's always on the lookout for danger. In this situation, it's as if your brain thinks, *Oh, I'm using my phone. Must be danger nearby!* Or *I'm heading to the library. That's where I go when there's trouble.*

So even if you think you're avoiding anxiety, your brain is working overtime to scan for signals of danger. Ultimately, your avoidance and safety habits increase the anxiety you feel.

Reason 2: You don't learn anything new.

If you never take a risk and try to do something differently, you can't learn anything new. If you don't take a risk and get on a bike, you'll never learn to ride it. If you don't get in the water, you can't learn to swim. It's the same with social anxiety. If you keep doing avoidance and safety behaviors, you can't learn that nothing terrible will happen in a feared situation when you don't do those behaviors. Moreover, you can't discover that something *good* could happen. You can't learn that you can actually handle uncomfortable social moments.

You also miss out on developing social know-how. That is, you don't learn the basic social skills we all have to know to make it in life.

Reason 3: You miss out on good stuff.

If you're busy avoiding or doing safety behaviors, you're likely to miss some important opportunities. You probably won't notice any evidence that shows people *do* like you. You probably won't realize that they *do* think you are funny, smart, good looking, and so on. For example, even though other kids liked Keto's drum playing, he couldn't feel the love. He was unable to learn that if he didn't do the safety behavior of changing out of his uniform, no one would make fun of him. In fact, those people were proud to know such a talented musician—dorky uniform and all.

Reason 4: You make the problem worse.

Whether we like it or not, we're social creatures. As social creatures, we naturally notice each other's behaviors and try to make sense of them. This includes any avoidance and safety behaviors we engage in. Unless they are indirect, these behaviors announce themselves to the world. If, for example, you avoid other people, they will notice and may start to avoid you, making the problem worse next time you need or want to interact.

Consider Amber's behaviors of avoiding talking to anyone she doesn't know well. Do you think other kids notice? Of course they do. And what do you think they make of her behavior? Even though Amber does those behaviors because she feels more comfortable and safer, other kids have their own interpretations. They might decide she is stuck up or a weirdo because she sticks to herself so much. If Amber didn't avoid the other kids, they probably wouldn't think much about her, one way or the other. But her behavior draws attention to her. Even if other kids originally had nothing against her, seeing her avoid them makes them want to avoid her too. In other words, Amber's behavior feeds the problem. Her anxiety is self-fulfilling. A behavior that was intended to guard against rejection leads to actual rejection.

LIST YOUR AVOIDANCE AND SAFETY BEHAVIORS

In this step of the CBT process, you are going to identify the avoidance and safety behaviors you use in each of your trigger situations. The reason you need to identify them now is so you will know what behaviors to refrain from doing when you build your exposure ladder in the following chapter.

Start with your trigger situations list. Find the trigger situations list you compiled in chapter 4. Make sure the column with your SUDS ratings is filled in for each situation. The situations on this list may be ones you avoid, ones in which you do safety behaviors, or ones with a combination of both kinds of behaviors. In this exercise, you will look at both avoidance and safety behaviors.

Obtain a set of index cards. You can use old-fashioned paper index cards or digital ones. There are a variety of index card apps available. You may already use one for schoolwork.

Write each of your trigger situations on the front side of a separate index card. Use one card for each situation. Depending on how many situations you have, you will build a little deck of cards.

Go through your cards. Using your index card deck, go through all of your trigger situations one at a time. You can do it like a game. Shuffle the deck and pick a card. Then pick your next card, in no particular order.

For each card, picture being in that trigger situation. Think about what you typically do before, during, and after that situation to deal with your discomfort. Ask yourself:

What avoidance behaviors do I use?

What safety behaviors do I use?

To get more specific, it can help to ask yourself for each behavior:

When do I do it?

Is it something I do or something indirect that I just think about doing?

Now draw a line down the middle of the back of each index card. Then draw one vertical line about a half inch to the left of the center line, plus another vertical line about a half inch from the right edge of the card. This should leave you with four columns. In the wide left column, record the *avoidance behaviors* you do in that situation. In the wide right column, record the *safety behaviors* you do. If you aren't sure whether a behavior is avoidance or safety or both, don't stress about it. Just put it on whichever side makes most sense to you now.

In chapter 6, you will use the narrow columns to record your SUDS rating for being in that trigger situation without doing each of the behaviors. For now, leave these columns blank. But be sure to hang on to your deck of cards. You will be using them again.

Martin's Report

Let's see how Martin assessed his avoidance and safety behaviors. He has his trigger situations deck of index cards in hand. To refresh your memory, here is an excerpt from his trigger situation list.

Trigger Situation	SUDS Rating
Wake up on school day and think about which classes I have	4-5
Walk past student lounge	6
AP English class	6-9

The first index card I looked at was for the trigger situation "Wake up on a school day and think about which classes I have." I started by asking how I feel and act when I wake up. I always feel uneasy until I know for sure I don't have World Politics or AP English. So I think about if I'll have those classes. I also think about if I'll have to walk by the student lounge. I try to plan my day to avoid hanging out in any crowded area.

I realized most of what's going on when I wake up is indirect avoidance. I'm just thinking about how to avoid the situations later. The main safety behavior I do after I wake up is put on clothes I think won't draw attention to me. I wrote all of these behaviors on the back of my index card. I added columns so I can do a SUDS rating for each behavior later.

Front of card:

Wake up on a school day

SUDS 4-5

Back of card:

Avoidance	SUDS	Safety	SUDS
Think about skipping class		Mentally check for trigger classes	
Think about avoiding crowds		Pick out low-key clothes	

The next card I pulled was "Walk past student lounge." Whenever I walk past the lounge, I try to figure out who's in there. If Spencer and Resse are there, I'm sort of okay. But if Sarah, Peter, Franco, or any other popular kids are there, I get pretty nervous.

Sometimes I rush to be early to my next class. That's an avoidance behavior because it keeps me away from the lounge. I also plan how I might escape to my locker or the library if I feel too stressed being around the student lounge. Other times I pretend I'm busy looking at my phone. I guess that's a safety behavior. But it also is kind of an avoidance behavior. Because if I keep my earbuds in and stay occupied with my phone, I can avoid eye contact. I wrote all my avoidance and safety behaviors on the back of my card.

Front of card:

Walk past student lounge

SUDS 6

Back of card:

Avoidance	SUDS	Safety	SUDS
Avoid eye contact		Rush by	
Think about avoiding crowds		Use my phone and earbuds	
Escape to locker or library			

    Then I pulled the card for AP English class. If it's a day I know for sure we'll read poetry out loud, I think about skipping class. I ask my mom to write a note so I can get out of class. Even though she won't do that anymore, I still ask. If I'm really freaking out, I fake being sick. I wrote those avoidance behaviors on my card.

    I think a lot about skipping AP English, but I usually end up having to go. To not attract attention, I sit in the back of the room. I act busy so Mr. Riordan won't call on me. I only talk when he asks me a question. Then I try to get it over as fast as possible. I give short answers and talk fast and not very loud. Those are all safety behaviors.

The minute I finish speaking in class, I start wondering if I said anything wrong or acted weird. I go over and over it in my mind. My voice sounds so squeaky and dumb, I'm sure the other kids think I'm an idiot. I hate it when Mr. Riordan says he likes my answer because then everyone looks at me. I start to shake and sweat. I put my hands in my pockets and pull up my hood so kids can't see me well. I can't wait to get out of that class. I realized I do a lot of safety behaviors in AP English. So I added them all to the card.

Front of card:

```
AP English Class

SUDS 6-9
```

Back of card:

Avoidance	SUDS	Safety	SUDS
Try to get excused from class		Sit in back	
Think about skipping class		Act busy	
Think about leaving class		Don't make eye contact	
Fake being sick		Talk fast	
		Talk in quiet voice	
		Put hands in pockets	
		Cover head with hood	
Keep going over what I think others thought of what I said			

FAQS

Q: *You said it doesn't matter, but I'm getting stressed trying to figure out the differences between my avoidance and safety behaviors. What should I do?*

A: Please don't stress about this! There is a lot of overlap between them. In fact, many therapists talk about these behaviors together when explaining how to do exposures. Some researchers consider them together when studying the effects of exposures. The reason I separate them here is so you can better understand your own behaviors. If I only call them "safety behaviors," you might miss behaviors you do to avoid or escape from trigger situations. If I only call them "avoidance behaviors," you might miss the ones you do for safety. I want to make sure you don't miss anything!

For example, take the behavior of not engaging in eye contact. Suppose you're approaching a group of kids and you're afraid they're going to tease you. You want to avoid them. So as you pass them, you avert your eyes. By not looking at them, you are engaging in an avoidance behavior. Now, suppose you're in class and you worry about being called on. So you adopt the safety behavior of always looking at the reading material and never at the teacher. You could say you're "avoiding" the teacher, but you could also consider this a way of keeping yourself "safe" in class.

The main point, however, is that this distinction doesn't matter when it comes to conquering social anxiety. What matters is that you identify the behaviors you rely on in trigger situations and then do exposures so you can be in those situations with less anxiety.

Q: *Are avoidance and safety behaviors ever okay to use? I mean, I kind of like some of them.*

A: In the broad scheme of life, some avoidance and safety behaviors are very healthy. That might surprise you, but think about it. Suppose an unrestrained wild tiger is approaching you. Avoiding that tiger would be your best move if you don't want your head bitten off. That's an example of a smart avoidance behavior, don't you think? Similarly, we wear seat belts to prevent serious harm in a car accident. Wearing your seat belt is a safety behavior that can save your life.

However, your question is probably really about whether it's ever okay to use avoidance and safety behaviors when there is no objective danger or threat to your safety. That's what happens in the case of social anxiety. Because you aren't in any real danger, those behaviors don't protect you at all. Rather—as you will see as you go through the five steps of the CBT Social Anxiety Relief Program—they keep you stuck in anxiety. So, no, you don't want to continue to use these behaviors. Stick with avoiding contact with wild tigers. And wear that seat belt.

Q: *I can't believe I could ever be in a trigger situation without doing some of my safety behaviors. How do I keep up my motivation when it seems like it will take forever?*

A: I understand. And I hear your question frequently. Sometimes when I'm working with a teen in my office, the numbers of behaviors seem overwhelming even to me. But I've learned to trust the CBT process. And I'm asking you to trust me: it won't let you down!

The most important thing is to get started. Don't waste time trying to determine how hard it will be or how long it will take. That will be different for each person.

Think about this from the perspective of what you've just learned: trying to gain certainty about the outcome of this process is really just another safety behavior. It's a way of protecting yourself from taking a risk and trying it out. It's a reason to avoid doing anything.

Once you start this process, your brain will start to learn, and you will gradually experience relief from your anxiety. With relief will come greater courage and motivation to give up more and more of these behaviors. The gains you make will be determined by how much hard work you're willing to put into the process. I suggest that when and if you feel overwhelmed, rather than fret about it, do something about it. I'll show you how in the next chapter.

CHAPTER 6

Building an Exposure Ladder

Now it's time for the next step on this journey: learning about, planning, and running exposures. Exposures are the single most effective way to relieve anxiety problems of all types, including social anxiety. In this chapter, you'll learn more about what exposures are and how to do them. You will take the first step in planning an exposure experiment: creating an exposure ladder.

Because one of the best ways to learn how to do exposures is to hear how other teens have done them, I've provided as many examples as possible. We've followed Martin as he sorted out his trigger situations and identified his avoidance and safety behaviors for each situation. In this chapter, you'll meet Alexa.

Alexa gets anxious in any situation where she has to speak with or in front of kids she doesn't know well, whether in the cafeteria, in class, or at a party. Alexa always brings lunch so she doesn't have to go into the cafeteria and interact with other kids. But she can't entirely avoid speaking in class—not if she wants to keep up her good grades.

For example, one day, before a social studies exam, Ms. Muñoz asks the class to form study groups of six students. Alexa ends up in a group with kids who all like to talk. This makes participation relatively easy: she can just sit there and nod her head a lot.

Then one student says, "I don't get the electoral college. What does it do?"

No one else knows the answer. So they all look at Alexa.

"Come on," prods the first student. "You know this stuff. Explain it to us."

"Yeah," says a second student, "quit holding out on us."

The others laugh. Alexa thinks she can hear one of the kids mutter "smarty pants." As she looks at them, all staring at her, waiting for her to speak, she freezes. In fact, Alexa does know the answer. She wrote a special report on the electoral college. But now she feels her heart racing and blood rushing to her head, and she can hardly get a word out.

"It's…it's," she stammers, trying to keep her voice from sounding shaky, "how the real votes get cast in an election."

As she speaks, her mind screams at her, *You're stupid! That's not even correct.* She hates that her voice isn't under her control and that the other kids might notice these physical signs of her anxiety. She is embarrassed that they will think she isn't poised, smart, or articulate.

We'll follow Alexa as she prepares for her first exposure experiment. But first let's start by talking about exposures in general so you have a better idea of what you'll be doing and why they are so effective.

WHAT ARE EXPOSURES?

In the English language, "exposure" means being in contact with something in a way that allows you to experience it fully. You can be exposed to many things: bad weather, poetry, the sun, gourmet food, a virus, new ideas, music, and more. Of course, there are degrees of exposure. And you might want some exposures but others not so much.

In CBT, "exposure" means coming into contact with a situation that triggers fear and anxiety, but that poses no actual danger, while refraining from engaging in avoidance or safety behaviors. As we discussed in the previous chapter, if you have social anxiety, you interpret various social situations as dangerous even when they are not. You may be uncomfortable in them, but these situations pose no actual danger.

You also know from the previous chapter how problematic and self-defeating relying on avoidance and safety behaviors is. You become trapped in a cycle of anxiety. What you want to do instead to break this unhealthy cycle is to expose yourself little bit by little bit to uncomfortable situations. Doing so gradually helps you get used to the situation and feel comfortable in it.

Doing exposures is like learning anything new: you break it down into manageable pieces and then practice until you get good at one piece before moving on to the next. For example, suppose you decide you're going to ski down a double black diamond slope for the first time; you probably need to master a single black diamond first. Or if your goal is to design a video game, you first need to learn how to code. It's the same with exposures: you start with the basics and you keep practicing as you work your way up.

No matter what you're learning in life, pain, frustration, awkwardness, thrill, embarrassment, exhaustion, exhilaration, and fear are all possible. So why would you put yourself in such a situation? Why would you tolerate some of these feelings? Probably because you want to reach whatever goal you set for yourself. You know that if you hesitate or hold back, you won't learn what you want to learn. So you practice. You take safe risks. You build your skills. You tolerate falls and missteps. You do all that because you know it's what is required to make progress.

Conquering social anxiety is no different. It might just feel different because you've never learned how to conquer it. Even if you saw a mental health professional for social anxiety, that probably didn't help unless it included exposures. To learn any new skill, you have to practice. And you need someone who can show you how. For example, if you want to learn how to do a double axel in figure skating, you need a figure skating coach. Similarly, with social anxiety, you need someone who can teach you how to do exposures. That's where I (and this book!) come in.

One reason the CBT process is effective is that it can be done gradually. It isn't a sink-or-swim operation, where you're just tossed into the deep end. If that were the case, most people would have a hard time mustering the courage to do exposures. It would be too hard. But if you start with easier exposures and work your way up, you will find you can handle it and do the exposures that will set you free from social anxiety.

In this chapter, you'll plan exposures that have a series of steps that let you gradually approach your trigger situations. Rather than get rid of all your avoidance and safety behaviors in one fell swoop, you'll approach them step by step and at your own pace. You will be in charge of the process. That also means you will have yourself to pat on the back every time you move toward a situation you fear and gain the sense of mastery and ease that is your goal!

WHAT YOU WILL LEARN FROM EXPOSURES

With each exposure you do, you'll learn about your ability to be in that situation. But you don't have to take my word for it. Here are some common things teens report learning when they do exposures:

1. "My worst fears didn't happen. If something did happen, it wasn't as uncomfortable as I thought it was going to be."

2. "When I don't do avoidance or safety behaviors, nothing bad happens."

3. "I can handle feeling some anxiety, and I feel okay again pretty quickly right after."

4. "What I worried will happen hasn't happened. I'm always surprised at how much easier an exposure is after doing it than I thought it would be before I started it."

5. "Other kids don't notice me as much as I think. Nobody has told me I'm a weirdo or anything bad like that."

6. "Even when I do something embarrassing, it's not so awful. Sometimes it's even funny to me."

7. "I'm not as inept socially as I think I am. Even if I'm nervous, I can have a conversation or ask or answer a question or two."

8. "Surprise! Other kids like to talk to me."

TYPES OF EXPOSURES

Before you start planning your exposures, it's helpful to know about the three main types: *in vivo exposures*, *imaginal exposures*, and *exposures to bodily sensations of anxiety*. Mostly you will do in vivo exposures, but the other types will help in some instances.

In Vivo Exposures

The Latin words "in vivo" mean "in the living." In other words, in real life, not in a laboratory setting or in your imagination. In vivo exposures are done in real-life situations. Your exposures will be designed so that you are in your trigger situation in real life, while not engaging in avoidance or safety behaviors.

Most of the exposures you do will be of this type. Here are three examples:

- One of Alexa's trigger situations is being in the school cafeteria. Her in vivo exposure will involve physically approaching or going into the cafeteria without doing her usual avoidance and safety behaviors.

- Troy feels anxiety being around boys he finds attractive and would like to date. His in vivo exposure will involve approaching or interacting with an attractive boy without doing his usual avoidance and safety behaviors.

- Chris is very uncomfortable if she has to sit in the front row in class. Her in vivo exposure will involve sitting nearer to or in the front row without doing her usual avoidance and safety behaviors.

Imaginal Exposures

Imaginal exposures are what they sound like: you *imagine* being in the trigger situation while not doing avoidance or safety behaviors. You mentally picture all the consequences you worry will happen. You use all of your senses (sight, hearing, smell, taste, touch) to imagine being in that trigger situation.

Imaginal exposures are helpful when your SUDS rating is too high to do an in vivo exposure. Often, they can be used before an in vivo exposure, as a first step to ease into an exposure. Imaginal exposures are also useful when a trigger situation occurs infrequently or almost never.

Here are imaginal exposures for the previous three examples:

- Alexa's imaginal exposure will involve mentally picturing herself going into the cafeteria without doing avoidance and safety behaviors.

- Troy's imaginal exposure will involve mentally picturing himself approaching or interacting with an attractive boy without doing avoidance and safety behaviors.

- Chris's imaginal exposure will involve mentally picturing herself sitting nearer to or in the front row in class without doing avoidance and safety behaviors.

You can try it quickly now, just to get a sense of it. For the purpose of this exercise, think of something *unrelated* to social anxiety that triggers fear for you. Could be a spider, snake, or mouse crawling up your leg, or a tornado touching down near your home. Once you have identified the thing, think about it happening. Imagine whatever you fear. And do this without reassuring yourself or doing any other avoidance or safety behaviors.

Let's say your SUDS rating is a 10 when you first imagine a snake crawling up your leg. Now, imagine the scenario ten different times. What is your SUDS rating each time? Most likely, your SUDS rating will be less than a 10 by the tenth imaginal exposure. The human brain, without fail, gets used to those things that initially cause us fear. Try it and see what happens for you.

Exposures to Bodily Sensations of Anxiety

Social anxiety is often accompanied by strong bodily sensations of anxiety. For example, in a trigger situation, you might experience shaking, sweating, hyperventilation (breathing too fast), chest tightness, lightheadedness, blushing, or trouble breathing. Some teens have such strong bodily sensations of anxiety that they experience panic attacks during which they find it hard to carry out their normal activities.

If you have these kinds of bodily sensations, you know how uncomfortable, even frightening, they can be. Because these sensations are so unpleasant, you may come to fear them in addition to fearing the trigger situation in which they occur. You might also worry that others will notice what's happening to you and judge you negatively. All of these fears can play into each other. Without realizing it, you may be facing anxiety on three fronts at the same time:

- Fearing judgment, rejection, ridicule, and discomfort in the trigger situation

- Experiencing strong physical sensations of anxiety that are in and of themselves distressing

- Worrying others will notice your physiological reactions and judge you as a result

For example, suppose Troy hyperventilates and sweats a lot when he's around boys he finds attractive. He very much wants to talk to boys he likes, but whenever he even thinks about doing so, he starts to feel his heart rate increase. That gives rise to worries about hyperventilating. As he worries, he begins to sweat profusely. In this case, Troy has three sources of fear: The first is his anxiety about interacting with attractive boys and being rejected or judged negatively. The second is having to deal with his distressing physical sensations. The third is his fear that boys will notice he's sweating and will reject him even more as a result.

If you have bodily sensations of anxiety that scare you, it can be helpful to do exposures to the sensations themselves. Technically speaking, we call these *interoceptive exposures*. That isn't as complicated as it sounds. "Interoceptive" simply means "arising in the body." So interoceptive exposures are just a fancy way of saying exposures to bodily sensations. The following are examples of interoceptive exposures:

- Hyperventilating on purpose
- Breathing through a narrow straw
- Running in place
- Doing push-ups (to bring on shakiness)
- Eating hot sauce (to induce blushing or sweating)
- Drinking a hot drink rapidly (to induce blushing and sweating)

When you do an interoceptive exposure, as with any exposure, you refrain from doing any avoidance or safety behaviors you normally might do to prevent or make those sensations go away. We'll talk more about doing this type of exposure in chapter 10.

YOUR EXPOSURE LADDER

You will build your exposure ladder in five steps. The first step is choosing the best trigger situation for your exposure. Second, you will tease out any sub-situations. This will make your exposure more manageable and help you target your particular fears. Third, once you've chosen your trigger situation (or sub-situation), you will give a SUDS rating to being in it without doing your avoidance and safety behaviors. Fourth, you will rank order your SUDS ratings. Finally, the fifth step is using those rank-ordered ratings to build a ladder for your first exposures. We will go through this process step by step, so hang in there if this sounds complicated.

Select a Trigger Situation

Your task is to select the situation from your trigger situation list for which you will do your first exposure(s). Recent research tells us that there is no particular order that's best for selecting which exposure to do first. However, I suggest you start with the trigger situation that has the lowest SUDS rating. This will allow you to ease into the process and work through it gradually.

Here are some tips for selecting your first trigger situation:

Start by taking out your deck of index cards. If you have physical cards, you can spread them out, with the front side up. If you're using digital cards, just look at the front of each card.

Identify the card with the lowest SUDS rating. Note that this is the rating you gave to the trigger situation when you first identified it, in chapter 4. It represents the level of anxiety and discomfort you feel in this situation, even when you *are* doing avoidance and safety behaviors. Later, you will consider SUDS ratings for being in trigger situations while *not* doing avoidance and safety behaviors. But for now, go with the ratings you already made.

What if several cards have low ratings? You may have two or three cards with the same or similar low ratings. If one doesn't stand out to you as a good place to start, you may want to consider how often each occurs. For example, Alexa's lowest SUDS ratings were for going to the school cafeteria, speaking to others at school, and going to a dance. The dance happened only a couple of times a year, so Alexa put that situation aside for now. Going to the school cafeteria happened every day, but it only happened once a day, whereas speaking to others at school happened several times a day. So she chose speaking to others for her first exposure.

Don't feel you have to avoid a challenge. You might be motivated to start with a trigger situation that has a higher SUDS rating. This could be a situation that really triggers you but that you feel is important to conquer ASAP. There's no reason not to tackle a situation with a high SUDS rating first. You can do that if you want. If it ends up feeling a bit too challenging, you can break that situation into smaller steps, or sub-situations, that lead up to the situation.

Consider sub-situations. You might be worried that even the situation with the lowest SUDS rating will be too uncomfortable. To help with that, you can break the situation down into sub-situations. Then you can start with the sub-situation that has the lowest SUDS rating. In fact, even if you aren't worried about whether the lowest SUDS rating will be uncomfortable, there are other reasons to identify sub-situations. Let's look at those now.

Identify Any Sub-Situations

You already worked with sub-situations when you made your list of trigger situations in chapter 4. Martin broke out the sub-situation of getting dressed from his primary trigger situation of early mornings. He did this because he realized a lot of worries added up to his main situation of early mornings. As you now know, breaking out a sub-situation can make it easier to understand and deal with the situation. Let's see how Alexa went about identifying her sub-situations.

Alexa's Report

The trigger situation I chose for my first exposure is speaking to others at school. I gave it a SUDS rating of 4-6. Knowing it was a range was my cue to think about sub-situations. So I thought about when it is harder and when it is easier to speak to others.

The biggest difference is how many people I have to speak to. Speaking in front of the whole class is the absolute worst. When I see everyone staring at me, I never know if my mind will go blank. That sub-situation has a SUDS rating of 6. However, a small-group discussion is less scary. When there are only five or six people, I can usually focus on one or two of them. And I try to get into small groups with a friend. So that sub-situation only has a SUDS rating of 4.

I also considered what else, besides the number of kids, affects my SUDS rating for speaking to others. One thing is the topic. I'm more confident speaking in front of the class when the topic is something I know well. For me, that can be anything involving facts. For example, speaking about history has a SUDS rating of 5, whereas speaking in French is at least a 6.

Another factor is how I feel about the teacher. Speaking in a class where I think the teacher likes me has a SUDS rating of 4 or 5.

After considering all these sub-situations, I decided to use the sub-situation of speaking in a small group for my first exposure. This will allow me to start with my lowest SUDS rating. Because we break into small groups in more than one of my classes, I'll have plenty of chances to run exposures.

Here are some tips for identifying sub-situations:

Review your trigger situations list. As you settle on the trigger situation for your first exposure, consider whether it would help to break it down further. You may already have done that when you compiled your trigger situations list in chapter 4. But give it another look, especially if you're concerned that its SUDS rating might be higher than you feel you can manage.

Be specific. Be as specific as possible about the situation in which you will do your exposures. Sub-situations allow you to design smaller rungs to climb on your exposure ladder. That makes the exposures feel more manageable, which in turn gives you greater confidence and makes you more likely to succeed.

Consider breaking down a ratings range. Pay special attention to SUDS ratings with a range, such as 2–3 or 3–5. You may want to identify a sub-situation at the low end of the range that would be an easier place to start your exposures.

Do SUDS Ratings

Now that you've selected the trigger situation for your first exposure, it's important to set yourself up for maximum success. The exposures you plan to do should feel doable—not too hard but not too easy either. To determine your comfort level, you need to assess your anxiety when not engaging in the avoidance and safety behaviors you usually use. You will do this using SUDS ratings.

So far, you've done SUDS ratings for each trigger situation and recorded them on the front of your index cards. However, when you made those ratings, you weren't yet thinking about being in trigger situations *without* doing avoidance or safety behaviors. Which means that you now need to revisit your SUDS ratings while keeping in mind how you feel when *not* doing those behaviors.

Grab the index card for your chosen trigger situation and fill in the columns on the back. For each behavior, estimate what your SUDS rating would be if you didn't use it. If you need to, go back to chapter 3 and review the instructions for SUDS ratings.

Alexa's Report

Let's look at how Alexa filled out her index card for the trigger situation of speaking in small-group discussions, which she gave a SUDS rating of 4.

Front of card:

Speaking in small groups

SUDS 4

Back of card:

Avoidance	SUDS	Safety	SUDS
Only speak when spoken to	4	Rehearse	7
Wait to speak	5-6	Not look anyone in the eye	4-5
		Nod a lot when other kids speak	5
		Make a short point	6
		Take notes to seem busy	4

  We're graded on our participation in small-group discussions. I want to be a good student, so I know it's important to speak. Plus, we're expected to speak without being called on. Ms. Muñoz said taking that initiative will prepare us for college. But I just can't do it, even though I feel like other kids stare at me when I don't speak up. So one of my avoidance behaviors is not speaking unless someone speaks to me first. I recorded a 4 for that in the SUDS column.

  My other avoidance behavior is waiting as long as I can for the best time to speak. If I have to speak up before any other kid does, I feel way more anxious. That has a SUDS rating of 5-6. As it is, before I get up the courage, another kid has usually said whatever I was going to say. Instead of speaking, I just nod my head to show I agree with that kid's point. If I can't do the safety behavior of nodding, my SUDS rating is a 5.

Another safety behavior I use in small-group discussions is not looking anyone in the eye. Not doing that behavior has a SUDS rating of 5. I also use the safety behavior of writing notes so kids will think I'm busy. Not doing that is a SUDS rating of 4.

Finally, I also rehearse in my mind over and over again what I want to say. I can't imagine speaking without rehearsing. I know I'd slip up or sound unsmart. So my SUDS rating for not rehearsing is a 7. I was amazed to see how much higher that rating is than the SUDS rating on the front of my card for speaking in small groups while doing my usual avoidance and safety behaviors. I marked all these new SUDS ratings on my card.

Tips for SUDS Ratings

Remember that your rating is for *not* doing the behavior. If this confuses you and you start to think of the rating as still representing *doing* the behavior, you can write in the words "not" or "don't" or "without." For example, if your card says "Avoid eye contact," you could change it to say, "Not avoid eye contact." If you are using digital index cards, you can easily create a new card with this change, if that helps you to be clear.

Expect higher SUDS ratings. Most or all of your new ratings will be higher than the rating you recorded on the front of the card. This is because now you're considering how you would feel *without* relying on your avoidance or safety behaviors. This shows why you rely on those behaviors in the first place: they work in the short run. But, as you now know, using them feeds and maintains your anxiety.

Rank Your SUDS Ratings

When you have completed your SUDS ratings for your trigger situation while not doing avoidance and safety behaviors, you will have a bunch of numbers on the back of your index card. You are going to use these numbers to set up the rungs on your first exposure ladder.

Rank SUDS ratings from lowest to highest. In other words, your lowest SUDS rating will be ranked #1, and your highest rating will have the highest rank. I suggest you mark the ranking number in front of the behavior listed on the index card. This way you won't confuse it with the SUDS rating for that behavior. You may also want to circle your ranking numbers to help distinguish them. If you are using a digital index card, you can use colors to distinguish your ranking numbers.

Differentiate behaviors with the same rating. If two behaviors have the same rating, consider which one is a bit more challenging, and give that one a higher rank order. If they are basically the same, give the one you feel like doing first the lower rank. The goal is to rank every behavior with a different number.

Combine ranks of avoidance and safety behaviors. So far you have kept separate columns for your avoidance and safety behaviors. The purpose of that is to help you understand why you are doing each behavior. Going forward, consider avoidance and safety behaviors together. For example, Alexa's ranked ratings for not doing her avoidance and safety behaviors in small-group discussions looked like this.

Avoidance	SUDS	Safety	SUDS
(1) Only speak when spoken to	4	(6) Rehearse	7
(4) Wait to speak	5-6	(2) Not look anyone in the eye	4-5
		(3) Nod a lot when other kids speak	5
		(5) Make a short point	6

Work quickly. Plan on no more than a few minutes to do this task. Don't get hung up on being too precise. Your SUDS ratings will shift downward after you start doing your first exposures, anyway, so your rank order will likely shift as well with time.

CREATE YOUR EXPOSURE LADDER

Now that you have the situation or sub-situation for your first exposure, you're ready to create your exposure ladder. I (and most CBT clinicians) use the metaphor of a ladder for exposures. A ladder allows you to climb one manageable rung at a time, from the bottom (easiest) to the top (most challenging). It is good to have four or five rungs on an exposure ladder, but there are no hard-and-fast rules about this. Some situations will need more rungs than others, depending on how challenging you find them. However, you should have enough rungs so no single step is too hard.

Create your ladder on a new index card or on a fresh piece of paper. Put each rung in order, based on your rank ordering of the SUDS ratings. Put the lowest rating at the bottom. For example, Alexa's ladder for speaking in small groups has six rungs. Her lowest rating is for only speaking when called upon, so it is the bottom rung. Note that her avoidance and safety behaviors are no longer separated at this point.

6. Rehearse (SUDS 7)

5. Make a short point (SUDS 6)

4. Wait to speak (SUDS 5-6)

3. Nod a lot when other kids speak (SUDS 5)

2. Not look anyone in the eye (SUDS 4-5)

1. Only speak when called on (SUDS 4)

What's next? You will begin to climb your ladder! Don't freak out, though, because the instructions in the next chapters will guide you rung by rung.

FAQS

Q: *I don't think I can ever get used to being in a trigger situation. I just don't think I can make that happen.*

A: I hear this a lot. The truth is, you *can* get used to being in a trigger situation. If you do repeated exposures, you will naturally become more comfortable in your trigger situation. That's one of the effects of exposures. Your anxiety will be reduced, and your SUDS rating will go down. This effect of becoming used to something is called *habituation*. It's a great effect to have!

Before 2015, CBT exposures focused entirely on lowering SUDS ratings. However, researchers realized that was problematic. The sole goal of lowering anxiety makes people feel that anxiety is bad and must be gotten rid of. This, in turn, feeds the fear of having even a little bit of anxiety. In fact, having a little anxiety is normal. So, instead of trying to eradicate all anxiety, it's important to learn that you can tolerate some amount of anxiety. If every time you feel some anxiety you panic and think it's bad, you will experience more anxiety.

If still you don't feel confident, you can try doing imaginal exposures before you try in vivo exposures. Or you can break down the exposure into a sub-situation you feel would be more manageable. For example, instead of not avoiding eye contact in social situations generally, you might stop avoiding eye contact as you walk past groups of kids at recess, for a start.

Q: *I like the idea of imaginal exposures. I've got a good imagination! Can I do all my exposures that way?'*

A: Imaginal exposures are great for some exposures, but you shouldn't rely on them entirely. The most common reason to use imaginal exposures is when you worry that an in vivo exposure would be too uncomfortable. Imaginal exposures are also helpful when it isn't practical for you to be there in person and when situations happen infrequently.

For example, say you're doing an exposure for going to a dance, but you're too uncomfortable to even set foot in the place where the dance is held. It also doesn't help that dances don't happen often. In this case, you could do the imaginal exposure of visualizing yourself at a dance without doing a particular avoidance or safety behavior. But don't stop there. Do an in vivo exposure when the opportunity arises, so you have a better chance of overcoming your social anxiety at dances.

Q: *How many exposure ladders will I need to do?*

A: That depends. You could do an exposure ladder for each of your trigger situations—that is, for each of your index cards. However, after you do one exposure, your SUDS ratings for your other trigger situations will most likely shift downward. And the process will get easier as you go along. The only way to find that out for sure is to start doing exposure experiments.

CHAPTER 7

Drilling Down on Your Fear

Congratulations on building your first exposure ladder and identifying the first rung on that ladder! You've done a lot of work to get to this point, and you're getting closer to trying out exposures—when you'll face your trigger situation *without* doing avoidance or safety behaviors. The thought of doing that might feel a bit scary, but you can handle it! Even if you have a little bit of doubt about that right now, you'll feel more confident when you have all the tools you need and know exactly what you're doing. This will make sure your climb is smooth and effective.

In this chapter, I'll give you an overview of the exposure process. I'll walk you through everything you need to do your first exposure. As part of this, I'll introduce you to the *downward arrow technique*, which will reveal the root fear in your trigger situation. What you truly fear may surprise you!

EXPOSURE EXPERIMENTS

I like to think of exposures as *experiments*, much like the ones you've done in science class. An experiment is a process of discovery. What will you discover by doing exposures? In a nutshell, you'll discover whether the outcome you fear when you don't do avoidance or safety behaviors is really as bad as you predict it will be. As the researcher, you'll learn how much anxiety is actually manageable when you face a trigger situation.

For example, suppose you're worried other kids will make fun of you if you say hi. I will teach you how to set up your exposure experiment so you can discover what actually happens when you say hi. If you don't do the exposure, you can't learn whether your fears are the same as, greater than, or less than what actually happens.

Or suppose you worry that you'll be too nervous to speak if you raise your hand in class and the teacher calls on you. Again, I'll teach you how to set up your exposure so you can discover whether you'll actually be able to say something when you are called on.

Are you shaking your head? Not so sure you'd learn anything helpful? That's okay! I'm not asking you to take my word for it. Instead, I'd like you to put on your lab coat and do the experiment. Bring an open mind. Make the discovery for yourself. You don't have to accept or agree with anything until it has been proven many times. And the person who is going to do the proving is no one else but *you!*

THE ELEMENTS OF AN EXPERIMENT

As you may recall from science class, when you do experiments, you use what's called the *scientific method*. In other words, you don't just fly by the seat of your pants. You use a carefully designed process that follows the flow shown here. The reason it's in a circle is that when you finish your first exposure, you will start the process all over again with your second exposure.

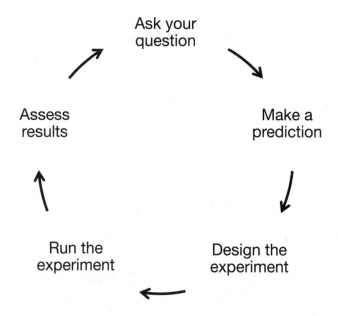

In the rest of this chapter, we'll cover the first two elements of the process: ask your question and make a prediction. We'll look at the three other elements in the next chapter.

Ask Your Question

All exposures answer the same basic question: *What am I most worried will happen in this trigger situation when I don't rely on my usual avoidance or safety behaviors?* You will ask yourself this question for each exposure you plan to run.

Let's revisit Juanita, the varsity soccer player you met in chapter 1 who was super anxious about making mistakes in front of others. Because of her anxiety, she is on the verge of quitting, even though she is an excellent athlete and has dreams of playing in college. Here is her first exposure ladder for the trigger situation of soccer practice:

5. Think about leaving practice early (SUDS 6)

4. Tell the coach my knee hurts, even if it doesn't (SUDS 5)

3. Get mom to tell coach I'm sick (SUDS 4-5)

2. Keep to myself at warm-up (SUDS 4)

1. Play extra carefully so I don't make mistakes (SUDS 4)

As you can see, this ladder lists the specific exposures Juanita will do despite her anxiety. Her first rung is to participate in soccer practice while refraining from playing extra carefully. That exposure has a SUDS rating of 4. The exposure of keeping to herself at warm-ups also has a SUDS rating of 4. However, she chose to give up her safety behavior of playing extra carefully as her first rung because she knows she can't play her best if she holds back.

She stated her question for this exposure as follows: *What am I most worried will happen at soccer practice if I don't play extra carefully and instead push myself to go for it?*

Make a Prediction

You will use the answer to your exposure question to make your prediction. A prediction is like a *hypothesis*—your theory about what will happen. In this case, you can think of it as your *fear-based prediction*. That's because it states what you fear will happen if you don't do a particular avoidance or safety behavior.

Juanita made this prediction: If I go to soccer practice and don't play extra carefully, I will feel super anxious and make mistakes, and all the girls will laugh at me. I could end up making so many mistakes that I get kicked off the team.

So that you can get a good feel for how predictions sound, here are some other examples.

Chan: If I walk around campus without using my earbuds, I will have to deal with other kids talking to me. I won't have a way to escape conversations, which will make me incredibly nervous. I will probably blush and start stuttering, and they will make fun of me.

Sophie: If I eat in front of others, I'll get so nervous that I will feel nauseated. I might even throw up. If I don't throw up, other kids will see that I'm shaking and think I'm weird. They won't want to be around me.

Kyle: If I answer a question in front of the class without using just one word or short sentences, I'll say something stupid and start to sweat. Everyone will see me sweating and freaking out, which will make me even more self-conscious and anxious. They will think I'm an idiot and that I don't know anything.

The four teens in these examples put a lot of thought into their predictions. And I want you to do that too. To help them drill down on their fears so they could create the most meaningful prediction, they used the downward arrow technique. Before we go further into the elements of planning your experiment, let me introduce you to the downward arrow technique. You will use the results of this exercise to help you turn your prediction into an effective experiment.

The Downward Arrow Technique

You might think that "the downward arrow" sounds like the name for a new dance move. But it's not. It's a series of questions about all the bad things you believe will happen in a trigger situation if you refrain from avoidance or safety behaviors. The worksheet shows a downward arrow between each question. You will follow these arrows as you answer each question.

The data you gather in this exercise will illustrate what we in CBT call your *fear structure*. That is, it will reveal the real root of your fears. You will see how your brain organizes your feelings and expectations each time you're in a trigger situation. Learning about your fears may feel scary at first, but knowledge is power. You're about to learn how to put this power to work in your favor.

To understand this technique, think about what it means for an investigator to "drill down" on something. You start out with a question. When you get an answer, you ask a more specific question about that answer. And then you ask an even more specific question to each answer that follows. In that way, you drill down.

To take an everyday example, suppose your dad asks, "What do you want for dinner?" You say, "Pasta!" So he asks, "What kind of pasta?" You say, "How about spaghetti?" He says yes and then drill downs: "Spaghetti with or without meatballs?" You say, "Without." He says, "Parmesan on top?" Like this, he continues to drill down. Similarly, the downward arrow technique refers to drilling down on the question "What will happen if I am in a trigger situation and don't use an avoidance or safety behavior?"

You may have asked yourself this exact question at times, but how far did you take it? Did you stop at "I just can't handle it" or "I'd feel too embarrassed" or "I'd feel so anxious I couldn't stand it"? It's easy to settle on the first, most obvious consequence that comes to mind. We tend to leave it at that and simply avoid the situation, because thinking more deeply can create anxiety. But if you stop there, that's where you'll stay. If you want to conquer your social anxiety, you need to go further.

The downward arrow technique challenges you to dig deeper and get to the root of what you fear most in a given trigger situation. This may sound kind of ominous, but most people get the hang of it fairly quickly. Are you ready to give it a try? You never know, what you find may surprise you!

To get started, download and print the Downward Arrow Worksheet from http://www.newharbinger.com/47056. Print out a fresh sheet for each situation. Or if you prefer, create a worksheet in your notebook or even on your phone. Here is the process to follow:

Pick your situation. Start with the first rung on your exposure ladder. Write down that situation at the top of your worksheet.

Think about being in that situation. Ask yourself, *What am I most worried will happen if I don't do an avoidance or safety behavior in this situation?* This is your first arrow.

When you begin to do this, you might find yourself answering something like, *If that happened, I'd just go to the restroom to calm down.* But that doesn't really answer the question, does it? Going to the restroom to calm down just substitutes one avoidance or safety behavior with another. To get a true answer, you need to clear away all the other ways you might cope or have tried to cope with being in that situation, then ask yourself, *What will happen if I'm in the trigger situation and I just have to be in it?*

Write down what you think would happen. On the worksheet, write down next to the first arrow what you think would happen. Your answer will be unique to you, but here are some typical outcomes teens give for their first arrow.

- I will feel awkward.
- I will feel super embarrassed.
- I will feel extremely anxious.
- I will tremble.
- I will blush.
- I will sweat.
- My voice will shake.

As you consider your outcome, don't overthink things. As long as your outcome is not an avoidance or safety behavior, there's no "wrong" answer. Just be honest with yourself and you'll be on the right track.

Move down to the second arrow. At this point, it might be tempting to think something like, *Yeah, okay, so I'd feel super embarrassed. End of story.* But not so fast—not letting yourself off the hook with a simple answer like this is exactly the point of drilling down! Rarely do we stop to think beyond our first notion of what will happen in a situation that feels threatening. Instead, I'm challenging you to keep asking, to drill down on your first outcome.

For the second arrow, reframe your question to ask what will happen if you feel or experience what you put down for the first arrow. For example, suppose your outcome for the first arrow was "I'd feel super embarrassed." Now you will ask yourself, *What will happen if I feel super embarrassed?*

Again, your outcome can't involve doing another avoidance or safety behavior. Rather, think about the consequence if what you thought would happen in the first arrow did happen. Then write that answer next to the second arrow on your worksheet.

Continue drilling down. The idea is to be persistent. Keep asking yourself questions until you start to tap into your deeper fears. You might look at those outcomes and think they're unlikely and even totally irrational. That doesn't matter; put them down anyway! These thoughts are important to uncover because they show how your brain is making you feel anxious. These deeper fears are driving your social anxiety, even if you don't realize it. So you want to uncover the irrational nature of your thoughts, not just stop at what you think your thoughts should be. Remember, you're doing this to understand your fear structure.

The Downward Arrow Worksheet has five arrows. There is no magic number for how many arrows it'll take to really drill down, but I suggest doing at least five arrows for each trigger situation. If you stop at two or three arrows, you likely won't learn about what your deeper fears are in a particular trigger situation. As you'll see in the example that follows, Juanita used eleven arrows, and she probably could have kept going from there.

Keep in mind that when you drill down there's no wrong answer. There's also no single answer and no single "real" fear. It's not like you'll drill down until you declare, "That's it! That's my real fear!" Theoretically, we all could probably drill down into our fear structures for the rest of our lives! The point here is to peel back your fear layers until you discover something new about yourself.

You also don't need to worry at this point about whether your deep fears are real or true. You will discover that by doing exposures. For now, just remember that it's common to have extreme fear-based thoughts. Even if you're unaware of these thoughts or know they're irrational, they are in your mind, warning that terrible things are about to happen and compelling you to engage in avoidance and safety behaviors. Using the downward arrow technique to shed light on your fear structure will begin to unlock their mystery.

Juanita's Downward Arrow Journey

Let's see how Juanita tackled the downward arrow process.

Situation: Practice before a soccer tournament without playing extra carefully

What will happen in this situation?

I will feel super anxious and probably make mistakes.

What will happen if... I feel super anxious and make mistakes?

Other girls will notice and start talking behind my back.

What will happen if... other girls notice and talk behind my back?

I will feel even more nervous and mess up more.

What will happen if... I feel even more nervous and mess up more?

They'll think I suck and should get off the team.

What will happen if... they want me off of the team?

I will feel so embarrassed and won't want to play at all.

⇓

What will happen if... I feel so embarrassed and don't want to play at all?

I will feel so awful I might even throw up.

⇓

What will happen if... I feel awful and throw up?

They'll make fun of me and tell everyone what a head case I am.

⇓

What will happen if... they make fun of me and tell everyone?

My playing will get worse and the coach will replace me with another player.

⇓

What will happen if... I get worse and worse and my coach replaces me?

That would change my whole life plan. Soccer is my main thing; colleges have already started talking to me.

⇓

What will happen if... my life plan changed and I couldn't get a scholarship?

I'd get super depressed and maybe never go to college.

⇓

What will happen if... I never went to college?

My life would be over. My parents, family, coaches, and all would be so disappointed in me. I might never be okay again.

At first, I didn't want to try this technique because I was afraid just the thought of not doing that safety behavior of playing extra carefully would make me more nervous in practice. Actually, that didn't happen. So I was relieved.

In my first downward arrow, I asked myself what would happen if I went to practice and didn't play extra carefully. It wasn't hard to answer that.

For the second arrow, I asked what would happen if I felt super anxious and messed up. Immediately, I knew what would happen. I'd do something to get out of the practice, like even fake twisting my leg. But then I realized that would be an avoidance behavior. So I had to drill deeper. I stopped and pictured the scene in my mind. That helped me realize that I worry other girls will notice me being anxious and will start talking behind my back. So I wrote that down.

I did a couple more arrows. I started to feel like I was going in circles just adding more arrows. Basically, feeling anxious makes it so others notice I'm a wreck, and when they notice I'm a wreck, that makes me even more anxious. I decided I needed to do more than five arrows to really understand my fear structure.

I'm glad I did, because I was able to get the hang of the downward arrow technique. When I did, I saw that my worries are pretty intense. I worry about what other girls think about me, and that has a way of snowballing in my mind. I futurize and catastrophize like crazy. One minute, I'm worried about girls talking behind my back. The next minute, I'm caught up in thinking my whole life will be over because I won't be able to play soccer because of my anxiety!

> My mom, my coach, and the other girls always say I'm a good player, but I don't believe them. I think they're just being nice. They remind me how many goals I've made and stuff like that. But I still don't believe I'm any good. Other times, though, I'm able to just have fun playing. Those days, I feel like my hard work is paying off. It's really weird that I worry so much about sucking at soccer, when mostly I play well enough to score and help the team.

FAQS

Q: *What happens if my fear-based prediction turns out to be true? What if the bad outcomes really happen like I think they will?*

A: In life, we can't completely avoid feeling embarrassed or uncomfortable in social situations. Everyone makes little errors! People with social anxiety often try super hard to do everything perfectly so they won't draw any negative attention to themselves. But holding yourself to unrealistic standards is a no-win proposition. It causes anxiety, puts others off, and messes up friendships. Most important, it's an impossible standard to meet. Much better to learn how to tolerate the inevitable, right?

One of the goals of exposures is to give you a chance to learn that other people don't pay close attention to errors you make. Overt criticism is rare.

Another goal is to allow you to learn that even if you are judged negatively for doing something embarrassing, such as spilling something or dropping an item, you can tolerate it. To this end, I often ask teens to do "planned embarrassment exposures." The rungs on their ladders include dropping items, spilling things, walking around with a stain on their shirt, asking the clerk at a cafe if they sell coffee, and so on. The exposure to such situations lets them learn that they can handle it.

Q: *How often should I use the downward arrow technique?*

A: Use it once for each trigger situation, or one worksheet per situation. Once you know the details of your fear structure for that situation and behaviors, you won't need to repeat it.

Some people make the mistake of using the downward arrow exercise every time they are triggered. They think doing so will help them see the irrational nature of their fears and thus make them feel better. Guess what? Used in that way, the downward arrow technique can become a safety behavior—a quick fix for anxiety. That isn't the purpose of the downward arrow exercise. So don't overuse it.

Q: *Just knowing that my fears are irrational hasn't helped me. How will doing the downward arrow technique help?*

A: Many teens with social anxiety do realize that their fears are either very exaggerated or irrational. But that alone isn't always enough. The purpose of the downward arrow technique is *not* to get you to see reason but rather to help you understand your fear structure. When you better understand how your brain works, you can design more effective exposures. You will be able to more accurately target the feared outcomes you predict. You'll see what I mean in the next chapter when you start to plan exposures for yourself.

CHAPTER 8

Planning an Exposure Experiment

Now it's time to get real! In this chapter, you're going to plan your first exposure experiment. We are going to go through all the logistics so you know exactly what your exposure will involve. As you learned in the previous chapter, an exposure is a way to test your fear-based prediction. The more your fear-based predictions are challenged and disproved, the stronger your new learning will be.

Before you run your exposures, you will fill out a Before the Experiment Worksheet. Go to http://www.newharbinger.com/47056 and download and print the form, or copy the questions onto a worksheet in your notebook or phone. The worksheet will prompt you to assess the following:

- What you plan to do
- What you're most worried will happen
- How you will know if what you predict actually happens
- How strongly you believe your prediction is correct
- Your SUDS rating
- Which avoidance or safety behaviors you might want to do
- How confident you are that you can do the exposure without doing avoidance or safety behaviors

Let's look at each of these items more carefully so you can fill out the worksheet and be prepared for your first exposure. I'd like you to think of the Before the Experiment Worksheet as the road map to your exposure plan. For this reason, I'll give two examples: one at the end of this chapter, filled out by Juanita, and one in the next chapter, filled out by Diya. This way you can see how it works for two different trigger situations.

WHAT YOU PLAN TO DO

Write your plan on the first line of your Before the Experiment Worksheet. Start by considering the specific conditions you need to include in your plan to test your prediction. To help work out these logistics, ask yourself the following questions:

Where and with whom do I need to do this?

When do I need to do it?

For how long do I need to do it?

How often do I need to do it?

Where and with whom do I need to do this?

Make your plan as specific as possible. Let's say walking in the hall at school is your trigger situation. If you pick a hall that is empty, you won't have a SUDS rating. Your SUDS rating will reflect how many kids are there, which types of kids, which part of the hall, and so on. Walking down the hall at lunchtime, when tons of popular kids are there, will give you a higher SUDS rating than walking between, say, the English classroom and the adjacent classroom where you have French. So pick your location accordingly.

Similarly, consider which people you want to increase your comfort level with. This will be related to the trigger situation for your exposure. Most likely, it will be your peers. But think carefully about who triggers you in that situation. Is it guys, girls, popular kids, handsome or pretty kids, jocks, older kids, kids you don't know well? Or teachers? If the situation is in a certain class, consider whether your SUDS rating is related to the number of students.

It is also important to find additional, similar situations in which you can practice. For example, plan to walk through various halls, not just the same one. Or, in addition to sharing your opinions in Social Studies class, share them in English class. This is where you can start to get a bit creative. You could plan to share your opinions with kids in the cafeteria at lunch and at home when your sister's friend is over for dinner. I know I said to be specific as you plan your exposures, but you can also be creative. Start out by being specific enough to target your fear structure, then expand to include related situations that have a similar SUDS rating. This way, you can get as much practice doing exposures as possible. You don't need to expand so far that you move into another rung on your exposure ladder, with a higher SUDS rating. But if you do and feel okay doing so, go for it!

When do I need to do it?

Exposures should be done every day, if possible. Look at your schedule to determine exactly when it would be best to practice. That might be determined by the situation. For example, Social Studies class and school assemblies occur at set times.

However, most exposures you plan won't come with a neatly set, prearranged time. In that case, waiting until you feel "in the mood" or until it feels "right" to do the exposure is problematic. To begin with, that's an avoidance behavior. Moreover, it will leave you feeling anxious and preoccupied all day. Instead, set a time that makes sense. For example, if your exposure is to refrain from pretending not to see the popular kids, think about when you're around those kids. Perhaps you could practice the exposure during recess or after school. Set reminders on your phone and commit to sticking with the plan you set.

For how long do I need to do it?

An exposure should continue past the point when you expect your predicted feared outcome to happen. This will vary, depending on the situation and the feared outcome.

For example, suppose your exposure involves being in the cafeteria when other kids are present, while not doing the safety behavior of pretending not to see the popular kids. Will one minute be enough to test whether other kids totally ignore or insult you? Or is five minutes going to be a better test? Set a timer on your phone if it helps you plan.

Or for an exposure that involves sharing your opinion in Social Studies class to see if your mind goes blank, think about how many times you need to share for that outcome to happen. Is raising your hand to share all it would take? Or will you need to plan to talk for a long time? And how long is long enough? If you're not sure, go by what seems average for other kids in class.

Plan your exposures to give you enough time to get a bit more comfortable being in that situation while refraining from avoidance and safety behaviors. A good rule of thumb for exposures is to stay in a trigger situation long enough or repeat an exposure enough times to allow you to learn something new.

How often do I need to do it?

You may not need that long to practice each exposure, but how often you do that exposure is important. Pick a situation that occurs frequently so you can make rapid progress. The more often you do an exposure, the sooner you'll feel less anxiety in your trigger situation. So commit to doing as many each day or each week as you can manage. There is no upper limit.

Of course, some trigger situations will occur less frequently than others. Or it may not be possible to do several exposures in that situation every day. For example, if your exposure involves sharing your opinion in Social Studies class, you can only do that on days when you have Social Studies. That being said, you can do more than one exposure per class.

Ideally, try to spread your exposures throughout each day. For example, do one in the morning, one at midday, one in the afternoon, and one in the evening. By spreading them out, you avoid the pitfall of trying to "get them over with" so you can be done with the whole business. In CBT, we call that "white knuckling" it. White knuckling is a form of avoidance and keeps you from learning as much as you can. It stops your progress in learning to tolerate a trigger situation.

Three Sample Plans

Here are some plans that the teens you met in the previous chapter committed to.

Chan is designing an exposure to talk with other kids while not doing the safety behavior of wearing earbuds. Because arriving at school without wearing his earbuds has the lowest SUDS rating, he made that his first rung. He decides he won't wear earbuds when he arrives at school five days a week. He's confident he can do that for at least ten to fifteen minutes before classes start. This will allow him to do the exposure enough times and for long enough to learn something new.

Sophie's exposure involves eating in front of others. For her first exposure, she decided to eat snacks at school in front of other kids. She still won't eat lunch in the cafeteria, because that has a higher SUDS rating than she can manage now. She will eat two snacks that are not too messy during the day, five days a week.

Kyle's exposure involves speaking in front of his class while not doing the safety behavior of responding only in one-word or short sentences. He has to clarify for himself how long his responses should be to not be considered "short." In this case, Kyle observes that most kids give about three sentences in a response. He also thinks about which classes to do exposures in. Kyle decides to do them in English and Math so he can do an exposure every day. He also speaks in short sentences in social situations with large groups of kids. However, that trigger situation has a higher SUDS rating, so Kyle leaves it for another rung on his exposure ladder.

If you remember Juanita and are wondering about her plan, hold on! We'll get to her full report soon.

YOUR BIGGEST WORRY AND HOW YOU'LL KNOW IF IT HAPPENS

The exposure you are planning now is designed to target your fears. And you know what your fear structure is from doing the downward arrow technique. But remember, your purpose is to prove the prediction you made. You want to know if what you predict will happen actually happens. So you need to get specific on this part of the Before the Experiment Worksheet: what are you most worried will happen?

For example, Chan is worried other kids will talk to him if he doesn't wear earbuds. The downward arrow exercise showed him that what he is most worried about is stuttering and looking uncool to those kids if he has to talk to them.

Sophie is worried that if she eats in front of others, she will do something—such as throw up or stuff too much food in her mouth and look sloppy—that makes her appear unattractive. She is most worried that kids will say she is gross or disgusting, and therefore won't hang out with her anymore.

Kyle is worried that if he doesn't speak in short sentences in class, he will say something stupid or mispronounce words, which will make him sweat and get more nervous. He is worried that if he does that, other kids—as well as his teachers—will think he isn't intelligent. He is most worried that he will get a bad grade and jeopardize his plan to get into college.

For your exposure experiment, decide how you can tell if your worry actually happens when you do your exposure. To do this, you can't use your emotions and anxious beliefs. We've already established that those beliefs are most likely not accurate. They're what got you into this predicament in the first place!

Instead of relying on your beliefs, you need to generate observable, objective evidence. What does that mean? *Observable* means that you can see the evidence with your physical senses. You can see (or hear) it happening. *Objective* means that it isn't just your personal view. Other people can also see (or hear) and confirm the same evidence.

When you're suffering from social anxiety, being objective about the outcomes you fear in trigger situations may not come naturally. It's a skill you may need to cultivate. To help you do this, I've listed some common examples of feared consequences. For each, I have provided the kind of objective evidence you need to be able to collect during your exposure experiment to answer your question of interest.

Feared Consequence	Objective Evidence
"She thinks I'm stupid."	She voices actual criticism of your intellectual work.
"Everyone thinks I'm weird."	Kids give you strange looks, which are observed by others.
"They won't talk to me because they think I'll be annoying if I join the conversation."	Kids ignore you when you say hi or talk to them directly.
"Kids will think my social media post is stupid and I don't do anything cool."	You receive negative comments on your post.
"I will feel so embarrassed, I won't be able to handle it."	You can't tolerate two minutes of feeling embarrassed and you leave.
"If I raise my hand in class, I'll stutter and people will laugh at me."	You actually stutter *and* hear laughter.
"If I go to the party and ask Maria to dance, she'll say no."	You ask Maria and she says no.
"If I tell Tom what I think about punk music, he won't like me anymore."	You tell Tom your opinion of punk music, and he breaks off his friendship with you.
"If I say hi to Jackson, he will think I'm a stalker."	You say hi to Jackson loudly and he ignores you or tells you to get lost.
"If I put on a bathing suit, everyone will make fun of my skinny legs."	When you wear your swimsuit, kids laugh, point to your legs, and say they're too skinny.

"I will fall off the balance beam and everyone will laugh at me."	You fall off and hear everyone laugh.
"I'll botch the experiment. When we get an F, my lab partner will blame me."	You actually get an F and your partner says it's your fault.
"No one will talk to me at the party."	Not a single person talks to you at the party even though you mingle.
"Sarah didn't text me today. She doesn't want to be friends anymore."	After Sarah doesn't text you, she no longer speaks to you.
"I'll be so nervous, I'll throw up at dinner and Marco will never ask me out again."	You actually throw up at dinner and then Marco doesn't talk to you anymore.
"If I try to eat in front of other kids, I'll feel so nervous I won't be able to eat."	You commit to eating a bite of your sandwich at lunch and you can't do it.
"If I post a selfie, I'll never get a single like."	You post a selfie and get no likes.
"If I walk in the school hallway alone, no one will say hi."	You walk the hallways between classes and every single person ignores you.
"If anyone hears me sing, I'll feel so humiliated, I won't be able to handle it."	You sing a little and leave school immediately.

THE STRENGTH OF YOUR PREDICTION

On the Before the Experiment Worksheet, you will also rate the strength of your prediction—that is, how strongly you believe that prediction. For this, you will use the BIP ratings you learned about and practiced in chapter 3. You finally get to use this tool from your toolkit!

The BIP rating is important because it gives you a basis for evaluating the success of your exposure. You will also see how much your fear-based beliefs change with each exposure you complete. As with any scientific experiment, you want to be able to compare your "before" with your "after."

For example, if you're Chan, how strongly do you believe you'll feel super anxious, stutter, and go totally blank so you're unable to say anything when other kids try to talk to you? If you're Sophie, how strongly do you believe you'll throw up and other kids won't hang out with you anymore when you eat a snack in front of them? Or if you're Kyle, how strongly do you believe you will freak out and other kids will criticize what you say when you speak in longer sentences in class?

Your rating will be in the form of a percentage from 0 to 100 percent. Especially for your first exposure, your rating will probably be 50 percent or higher. If it's not that high, that means you already know with some certainty that what you worry about most won't actually happen. For example, suppose Chan is only 20 percent certain he'll get anxious and stutter. If he runs his experiment and doesn't get anxious or stutter, he may not be surprised. But he's still learned something. Plus, he may be ready to move on to his next exposure sooner than he expected.

Note that even if you logically believe your feared outcome will only happen 20 percent of the time, you may still have a higher SUDS rating than you think you should. That's normal. And it's why you want to run your planned exposure experiment.

YOUR SUDS RATING

You already have a SUDS rating for the first rung of your ladder. You used that rating to determine your first rung. However, as you decide exactly what your first exposure will be, you'll want to reassess your rating. When you are close to doing the exposure, it may seem scarier than when you were just thinking about it. Or you may realize an exposure will be easier than you imagined. Either way, you want to make sure you don't make it too hard or too easy.

For example, Chan has a SUDS rating of 4 for walking on campus without wearing earbuds around other kids. If he designs an exposure in which he resists wearing earbuds in the first fifteen minutes of school, knowing he can still use them the rest of the day, his SUDS rating will still be a 4. However, if Chan were to stop his earbud use cold turkey all day, his SUDS rating would jump to a 6, which would likely make the exposure too hard.

On the other hand, if your exposure doesn't target your fear structure, it will likely be too easy. Suppose Kyle chooses PE class as the place to do his exposure of talking in front of the class while not doing the safety behavior of using short sentences. The problem is that he doesn't need to speak much in PE, so his feared outcome of kids thinking he's stupid has a much lower chance of playing out there. That's because this exposure doesn't target his fear structure. In fact, when he reassesses his SUDS rating, he sees that PE class is only a 2. Therefore, he decides to stick with English and Math classes.

The key is to design your exposure so it feels manageable. Continue to refine it and to reassess your SUDS rating until you feel comfortable about what you're about to undertake.

YOUR TEMPTING AVOIDANCE AND SAFETY BEHAVIORS

The Before the Experiment Worksheet asks you to identify and write down the behaviors you might feel tempted to engage in during your planned exposure. You likely know what these are because you designed your experiment to refrain from doing them. But not so fast! You might find yourself tempted to do new avoidance and safety behaviors, besides the ones you're planning to refrain from.

For example, Chan is refraining from doing the safety behavior of wearing earbuds when he arrives at school. He knows he'll be tempted to put his earbuds in if he has to walk through a big bunch of kids right by his locker. When he thinks more about it, he realizes he might also be tempted to do his avoidance behavior of imagining he's playing a video game.

Sophie knows she might be tempted to avoid eating the two snacks she has committed to eating in front of other kids. She figures that she might be tempted to eat them after school, on her way home. Or, if she's really hungry, she might be tempted to eat them in the bathroom, where no kids can see her.

YOUR CONFIDENCE LEVEL

The final question on the Before the Experiment Worksheet asks you to gauge how confident you are in being able to *not* engage in any avoidance or safety behavior. This is an important step for your success.

Rating your confidence level gives you a third way (in addition to your BIP rating and your SUDS rating) to make sure your exposure is on target. If you have high confidence that you can do the exposure without doing avoidance or safety behaviors, you have likely planned an effective experiment. However, if your confidence is medium or low, you should consider adjusting your plan to make your first exposure more manageable.

Juanita's Report

This chapter has covered a lot of details. Here, to put them all together for you, is Juanita's Before the Experiment Worksheet and her report describing how she filled it out.

What I plan to do: **Go after the ball whenever I have the chance in soccer practice.**

What am I most worried will happen? **I'll get super anxious and stumble or trip over the ball. The girls will laugh at me and talk about me behind my back. They'll say I don't belong on the team.**

How will I know this happened? **I'll hear the girls laugh at me. I won't know right away if they talk about me behind my back. But I'll worry about it and eventually I'll find out that they want me off the team.**

How strongly do I believe my prediction is correct (0–100%)? **50%**

What will my SUDS rating be? **5**

Which avoidance or safety behaviors might I want to do? **Think about leaving practice; not go for the ball every time I can.**

How confident do I feel that I can do the exposure without doing avoidance or safety behaviors?

High? Medium? Low? **High**

For my first exposure to target my fear structure, I need to find out what happens when I don't use the safety behavior of playing extra carefully.

I thought about exactly what I'm willing to do for the exposure. When I'm being extra careful, one thing I do is not be very aggressive. If another girl is closer to the ball, I let her take it. If a girl is coming at me when I have the ball, I give it up immediately. And I never, ever do a header.

When I thought about not doing any of these safety behaviors, it seemed like too much. That would have a SUDS rating of at least a 6. So I decided to focus on getting to the ball more quickly. When I have a chance to get the ball, I won't play it safe. I'll be more aggressive. However, I still won't do any headers.

We practice for 45 minutes two times a week. So picking the time and place and duration was easy for me.

If I do this exposure, I honestly think the girls will realize I suck and want me off the team. That's my prediction. I know it's fear based, but I'm willing to test it out. I'm glad the CBT process is pushing me to be objective. Normally, if you asked how I know the girls want me off the team, I'd say something like, "It's obvious" or "I just know." But now I'm going to look for real evidence. Like, I'll know if they want me off the team if they tell me.

I'm 50 percent certain my prediction will happen. I guess the other 50 percent believes it might not happen even if I get anxious and make mistakes.

My original SUDS rating for my first rung was 4. But after thinking through all the details, I upped it to a 5. Still, I'm highly confident I can do this.

FAQS

Q: *What if other kids find out that I'm planning exposure experiments? Will they think I'm even more weird?*

A: The brain of someone with social anxiety is primed to focus on fears of being judged and ridiculed by others, so this question doesn't surprise me. Of course, you have no reason to share with anyone that you are working on your social anxiety. You can keep it to yourself or just among members of your family.

That being said, you're not alone. With as many as 10 percent of teens experiencing social anxiety, I think it's fair to say that anxiety is a natural part of life in today's demanding world. You have to maintain a good GPA and prepare for SATs and ACTs, you want to make friends and have romantic interactions, and so on. All of these can trigger anxiety. I'll bet at least one friend has shared with you that they see a therapist. There is nothing to be embarrassed about or ashamed of when it comes to the need to talk openly about how you feel. Similarly, there's nothing embarrassing or shameful about doing exposures. If another kid learns you are practicing exposures, they'll most likely think you're cool for being brave and taking action. They might even want to learn about how to do them!

Q: *I'm having a hard time coming up with objective evidence. I worry other kids think I'm annoying and boring. But I don't live in their heads. How can I know what they really think?*

A: You're right. None of us can know for sure what someone else thinks about us. Since we can't know, believing we *must* know sets us up for failure. Instead, you can develop the ability to tolerate not knowing for sure. That's where objective evidence comes in. It may not give you certainty, but it does give you valuable information.

I suggest you look for data indicating that others are okay with you. For example, notice when kids make small talk, sit next to you in class, ask your opinion, say hi during recess, and so on. If a kid tells you directly that you're annoying, that's objective evidence of your fear. If kids ignore you when you make a comment (be sure it's not because you spoke quietly and they couldn't hear you), that's objective evidence. Or if kids walk away when you say something, that's objective evidence. Rely on that, not on what you imagine is happening.

Q: *What if I don't feel confident that I can do any of the exposures I planned?*

A: First, consider if you've taken on more than you can manage. Take a SUDS rating and, if needed, adjust the exposure so it's a bit less challenging.

Some people think knowing that their fears are irrational will make doing exposures easier. But it doesn't work that way for most people. You may think, *I can do this! My fears are totally not going to happen.* But then your emotions surprise you. When you actually approach the trigger situation, you don't feel as confident as you did when you were just thinking about it. You temporarily lose objectivity, which makes it harder to take the plunge.

If this happens and your confidence drops, try a series of imaginal exposures before committing to the in vivo exposure. The more exposures you can do, the better. And imaginal exposures pack a powerful punch.

CHAPTER 9

Running an Exposure Experiment

Ready, set, go! Now you're ready to run your first exposure. You will execute the plan you made in the previous chapter. What might this look like? Here are a few examples:

- You might say hi each morning to two kids you don't usually speak to.
- You might raise your hand once in each English Language Arts class.
- You might go with a friend to a party.
- You might make eye contact with kids as you walk between classes.
- You might use a public restroom when you're at a store or school.
- You might stay in the kitchen and not go to your room when your brother's BFF is visiting.
- You might not check your phone during recess.

These are just some examples. What you specifically choose to do isn't necessarily on this list. But it will reflect what you've already learned about the trigger situations that spark social anxiety for you. Your exposure experiment will be unique to you, and you will agree to it fully voluntarily.

WARM UP WITH IMAGINAL EXPOSURES

In chapter 6, you learned about imaginal exposures as a stepping-stone for in vivo (real-life) exposures. You tried one for something unrelated to social anxiety—such as a snake crawling up your leg—and hopefully you got a sense of how it could be helpful.

Imaginal exposures are effective because they allow your brain to acclimate to the scary feelings you have. That way, your fears can lose some of their power before you start in vivo exposures. This also helps you learn that you can tolerate at least just thinking about the outcomes you predict will occur if you are in a trigger situation.

Think of warm-up imaginal exposures as a dress rehearsal. You don't have to do any rehearsing if you're ready for an in vivo exposure. And it's not a required step for every rung on your exposure ladder. However, here are some reasons you might want to include this step:

- Your SUDS rating for this exposure is a bit higher than you're comfortable with.
- You're a bit hesitant in general to start doing in vivo exposures.
- You have a good imagination and can easily visualize things.
- The trigger situation for your exposure doesn't occur every day.

Even if you decide against doing an imaginal exposure now, please read this section. It contains information that isn't repeated elsewhere.

Let's see how Diya got things rolling, and then I'll give you some tips for your own imaginal exposure.

Diya's Report

Diya's trigger situation is being around kids she doesn't know super well and needing to make idle chitchat. Her main safety behavior for that situation is to use her BFF Ellen as a buffer. She texts Ellen before breaks and lunch, and even between classes, to make sure they can be together. If Ellen isn't around, Diya avoids or escapes from any situation that might lead to the need to talk to kids she doesn't know well.

The first rung on Diya's exposure ladder is to go to morning break without first texting Ellen. Her plan for this exposure is to spend five minutes of the break near the benches under the oak tree. Her prediction is that she won't know what to say or will say something stupid when she is there without her BFF; either way, other kids will think she's a loser. Here's her report on doing an imaginal exposure for this situation.

> Going to morning break alone without texting Ellen sounded too scary for my first in vivo exposure. So I decided to do it imaginally first. That has a SUDS rating of only 3, compared with a 5 for doing it in real life at school.
>
> I did the imaginal exposure alone in my room, so no one would disturb me. I started by picturing myself walking from my locker to the benches. Just doing that without my BFF gave me a SUDS rating of 1. When I imagined walking past all the kids, my SUDS went up a little more.
>
> Even walking to the benches in my mind, I automatically started to want to know where Ellen was. I wanted to look for her because I couldn't text her. I know looking for her is a safety behavior, so I didn't do it. In my mind, I kept walking. I didn't imagine talking to anyone on my way to the benches.

When I got to the benches, I realized choosing where to sit would be a big deal if Ellen wasn't there to sit with. I imagined sitting in an open spot that wasn't right next to anyone. That made my SUDS rating go up to a 3. I pictured more kids gathering, joking, and laughing. I just sat there and imagined myself eating the snack I'd brought with me, feeling uncomfortable.

As soon as I thought the five minutes for the exposure were about over, I visualized myself getting up from the bench. The second I was on my way back to my locker, even in my imagination, my SUDS rating went back down to 1.

That exposure wasn't as bad as I thought it would be. I never had a SUDS rating of more than 3. I felt more comfortable than I expected.

It didn't take very long to imagine what would happen during a five-minute exposure. So I did it two more times. Each time, I didn't visualize talking to any kids. After that started to feel easy, I made it a little harder. For my fourth exposure, I imagined sitting down next to Karen, who I know a little and who seems nice. I imagined she said hi and I said hi back. We both ate our snacks and watched everyone goof off. I was a bit worried she'd try to chitchat, but since she's shy like me, I was comfortable enough. After that, I said I had to go to English and said bye.

I did ten imaginal exposures total. I picked up speed. The whole set took just five minutes. Now I'm more confident about doing my first in vivo exposure. My SUDS rating for that has come down to a 4. I'm ready!

Tips for Imaginal Exposures

Find a spot where you won't be disturbed. You will be doing this exposure in your own mind, as if you were physically in the situation. So you want a quiet place where you can sit by yourself for about ten minutes.

Imagine being in the trigger situation while not doing any avoidance or safety behaviors. In your mind's eye, imagine the physical location and the person or people in your trigger situation. Use as many of your five senses (seeing, smelling, hearing, tasting, and touching) as you can to vividly imagine being there. What do you hear? Are people talking? Is there background noise? Do you feel the warmth of the sun or the chill of a cool day? Pay attention to your full experience, including any temptation you feel to engage in an avoidance or safety behavior.

Imagine your feared outcome. If your trigger situation has a particular event—for example, something another person says or does, or something you would say or do—imagine that happening. Imagine that whatever outcome you fear will happen is happening.

Yes, I want you to go after what you fear most: kids laughing at you, ridiculing you, ignoring you, talking behind your back. Go for the worst-case scenario. Ask yourself: *What thoughts are going through my mind? What emotions am I feeling? What physical sensations am I experiencing? Is my heart racing? Am I sweating? Shaking? Breathing rapidly?* If you fear you will have any of these sensations while being in the trigger situation, imagine them happening to you now.

Keep a running SUDS rating. If you're worried about your anxiety going up, remind yourself that it will probably happen at first, and it's a good thing! Because if an exposure doesn't bring on a higher SUDS rating, it won't be helpful. If you start to imagine doing an avoidance or safety behavior to lower your SUDS rating, don't. Imagine you are following through with your commitment to yourself to *stop doing those behaviors*. Stick to it!

Use this as a practice run. You won't need to complete Before the Experiment and After the Experiment Worksheets for imaginal exposures. You'll use SUDS ratings, but you won't use BIP ratings or formally assess the results of your prediction—that comes next, with your first in vivo exposure.

RUN YOUR EXPOSURE EXPERIMENT

You're now ready and set. Like an athlete, you've done all of the training you need to do, and it's time to go!

When you planned your exposure experiment in the previous chapter, you clarified all the logistics you need to carry it out. And you practiced those by doing some imaginal exposures. Even so, it's a good idea to review your plan now, before you get started.

By now, you should be very familiar with the Before the Experiment Worksheet that you filled out in the previous chapter. You may want to make slight changes to your worksheet, based on your experience with imaginal exposures. For example, Diya learned during her imaginal exposure that where she sat made a difference in how hard the exposure was. So she will factor in the effects of sitting next to different kids in future exposures.

Also double-check your SUDS rating. It may have gone down after doing imaginal exposures. Also check your prediction, the percentage you believe your prediction, and your confidence level. All of these should reflect what you feel now. Your beliefs and SUDS ratings may have already started to change!

Diya's First Exposure

Take a look at Diya's Before the Experiment Worksheet, then read about how her experiment went.

What I plan to do: Walk by myself from my locker to the benches, sit down, and eat my snack.

What am I most worried will happen? Ellen won't be around and I will be alone with kids I don't know. Someone will start to chitchat and I won't know what to say. I'll say something they think is pathetic.

How will I know this happened? I'll see the kids staring at me. I won't be able to say anything. Or I'll say something, and the kids will laugh at me.

How strongly do I believe my prediction is correct (0–100%)? 60%

What will my SUDS rating be? 4

Which safety or avoidance behaviors might I want to do? Text Ellen. Look for her before I go to the benches. Leave the benches and go to my locker.

How confident do I feel that I can do the exposure without doing avoidance or safety behaviors?

High? Medium? Low? High

After my imaginal exposure, I did the same thing in real life. I started my exposure at the end of Geometry class, when we go for morning break.

Immediately, as I picked up my phone, I wanted to text Ellen. It felt weird not to do it. I even worried she might think something was wrong with me because I always text her. I had a SUDS rating of 4, just knowing I couldn't count on Ellen to be with me today. But I also knew that was the point of the exposure. I wanted to test my prediction that other kids will see me as a loser if I'm by myself and say dumb stuff. My BIP was 60 percent. I believed my prediction was probably correct. Which is okay: I could handle it.

My plan was to do the exposure for five minutes. As soon as I left class, I picked up my snack from my locker. It took two minutes to walk to the benches by the oak tree. While I was walking, my mind went into overdrive about whether any kids at the benches would try to chitchat with me. Nobody tried to talk to me while I was walking alone. That kind of surprised me and also relieved me a little. My SUDS rating was a 3 as I was walking. I got all sweaty with worry about what would happen at the benches.

I was really tempted to text Ellen after all. I thought if I didn't actually ask her to meet me, but just texted that I was at the benches, that wouldn't count as a safety behavior. But I knew it would be cheating. In the end, I didn't text her.

When I got to the benches, I was glad I'd done the imaginal exposure. That gave me a heads-up about where to sit when Ellen wasn't with me. Luckily, there were several open seats. I sat down at the far end of the bench, near the oak. One guy was sitting at the other end. He didn't seem to notice me.

As I got busy eating my snack, a few more kids came over. None of them really seemed to care that I was there. So I relaxed just a little. My SUDS rating was a 3. Time seemed to go slower than in my imaginal exposure. Even so, the other kids never really looked at me. Since they were ignoring me, I didn't feel any need to rush out of there. My SUDS rating stayed around a 3 for a while. It even went down to a 1 a couple of times. That surprised me, since I thought I'd be really uncomfortable for the entire exposure.

I'm planning to do the same exposure again tomorrow. I can do it twice—at morning break and at afternoon break. Based on today, my SUDS rating has gone from a 4 to a 3 for this trigger situation. I think I've got this.

After Diya did her first exposure, she completed an After the Experiment Worksheet.

Did what I was most worried would happen occur? **No.**

What did happen? Was I surprised? I was the most anxious as I was walking from my locker to the benches. But when I sat down, nothing bad happened. Nobody talked to me. They just did whatever they were doing. I was surprised I didn't feel weird and other kids weren't looking at me like I was a loser. A few other kids were sitting by themselves for part or all of the time, doing different things.

How strongly do I believe my prediction was correct (0–100%)? **10%**

What was my actual SUDS rating? **3**

What did I learn? It was like with my imaginal exposure—I realized the other kids don't really care what I do. Kids just gather with their usual friends. I learned that what I worried would happen didn't happen, and my mind does that to me a lot.

WHAT DID YOU LEARN?

As you can see, what Diya was most worried about happening didn't actually occur. She ran a scientific experiment, and she achieved a data-driven result. Her prediction proved to be incorrect: her BIP rating went from 60 percent down to 10 percent. In other words, she no longer strongly believed in her fear-based prediction for the trigger situation of being around kids she doesn't know well.

Diya had predicted that other kids would want to chat with her and that she would become so anxious she'd say something others would judge to be pathetic. None of this happened. In fact, she learned that other kids generally went about their business without paying attention to her. She was surprised at how much easier and more natural being in that situation felt than she had expected. She also learned that what her mind tells her is going to happen isn't always what happens, and that she can too easily fall for these kinds of thinking errors. She will take this new knowledge into future exposures and also into regular life.

The goal of every exposure is for you to learn something new. Therefore, the final step of every exposure experiment you run is to record your results. Fill out an After the Exposure Worksheet as soon as you can after you have run your first exposure. Go to http://www.newharbinger.com/47056 and download and print the form, or copy the questions onto a worksheet in your notebook or phone.

You don't have to fill out separate worksheets for each separate exposure. You will often do more than one exposure in a day. So you can't realistically do worksheets for all of them. But you can update your worksheet answers as you do more exposures and your answers change.

Remember that you have been following the scientific method. You made a prediction, and then you gathered objective evidence to see if your prediction bore out. You are now in a position to evaluate whether your fear-based prediction was accurate. To evaluate your prediction, compare your answers on the before and after worksheets. The first question on the After the Exposure Worksheet asks you directly whether what you predicted would happen did happen. Even if your answer is no, it didn't happen, take the time to compare the two worksheets more closely. Did what you feared most actually happen? Was it as bad as you predicted? Were you able to tolerate your anxiety more easily than you thought? Did your thoughts about the situation change? Careful consideration of these questions will help consolidate the new learning in your brain.

Please don't skimp on your attention to this step. Remember, people with social anxiety tend to overfocus on the negative outcomes and undernotice the positive ones. If your brain, through no fault of your own, is doing this over and over in social situations, you are training it to remember the bad stuff and ignore the good stuff. Instead, by solidifying these new lessons in your brain, you increase the chances that the next time you're in a similar situation, you will remember that things were okay. Your brain won't jump to unlikely negative outcomes, as it was used to doing.

Seeing in writing the difference between your fear-based prediction and what really happened can also be very motivating for future exposures. In the next chapter, you will consider whether you have learned enough from the exposures you've done to warrant moving on to the next rung on your exposure ladder.

FAQS

Q: *I've done a few exposures, but I'm not feeling any better about my trigger situations. How many more exposures do I have to do?*

A: Usually, exposures need to be practiced several times for your brain to learn. However, this varies from person to person. Some people require very few exposures, and others require more. If you've done lots of exposures and aren't feeling less anxiety in the trigger situation, a couple of things could be happening. One is that you could be doing avoidance or safety behaviors during your exposures. The other is that you haven't yet done enough exposures.

Review the avoidance and safety behaviors you listed on your Before the Experiment Worksheet, particularly those you *might be tempted to do*. Did you do any of those, even without realizing it?

Also consider other avoidance and safety behaviors you typically do but may not have included on your worksheet. Did you wind up doing any of these behaviors without realizing it? Often, people come up with new avoidance or safety behaviors when they feel pressed. Have you traded one avoidance or safety behavior for another? If you have, correct course and give up the new behavior too. If you can't think of any behaviors that might be impeding your exposures, then you need to do more exposures.

Q: *What if I don't feel very confident that I can really follow through with an exposure I planned?*

A: If your confidence level is only low or medium, I suggest doing more imaginal exposures. Do fifty of them and then reevaluate your confidence level. That usually does the trick. If, however, you still lack confidence, you can try doing the imaginal exposures while you are in the place where the trigger situation occurs. For example, Diya could walk from her locker to the benches when no other students are around (such as after school) and imagine that they are. Or you can make the exposure you have planned easier by breaking it down into sub-situations.

CHAPTER 10

Getting the Most from Your Exposures

Remember Steffie from earlier chapters? When we left her, she'd finished her first exposure and was eager to climb more rungs on her ladder. Now she's successfully done exposures for several more rungs, including for the trigger situations of walking around campus and of talking to kids she doesn't know well, without doing her avoidance and safety behaviors. The rung for lunchtimes seemed too easy in comparison, but she did it anyway, knowing that more practice is better.

Next up for her is parties. That's the trigger situation we initially met her in, when she bugged out on going to the pizza party at Elliott's house. Now she's been invited to her friend Lola's birthday party. She's decided to use it to run an exposure. But it wasn't just her success with previous rungs on her ladder that inspired Steffie to do this exposure. She's also been working on her social skills. At the party, the social skill of starting conversations will make it easier for her not to engage in her avoidance behavior of standing outside groups and not saying anything. Here's how it works for her.

When Steffie arrives at the party, she sees that Lola is busy with some friends. That gives Steffie an immediate SUDS rating of 3. The thought of ducking out before anyone has noticed crosses her mind. But she reminds herself that the thought of leaving is a safety behavior. She knows a spike in her SUDS rating is to be expected. She tells herself that this is an exposure and she can handle it. So she goes out to the patio, where she spots Elliott. She walks up to him and starts a conversation.

"Hey. What're you drinking?"

"Fruit punch," he says with a smile.

Steffie relaxes a little, seeing that Elliott isn't ignoring her. She continues, "Is it good?"

"It's awesome! I heard Lola say her sister made it."

"Really, her little sister?" Steffie relaxes more as she realizes they can discuss something as simple as the punch. Gone is her impulse to duck out. She's on her way with this new rung on her exposure ladder.

In this chapter, we'll look at how you can go about climbing more rungs on your ladder. I'll also give you some tips for creating the most effective exposures.

While exposures are the most useful technique for dealing with social anxiety, they aren't the only thing you can do. Like Steffie, you can build your social skills as a tool for reducing social anxiety. The second half of this chapter covers some key social skills. We'll talk about starting conversations, small talk, switching topics, and inviting someone to do something with you. We'll also cover some assertiveness skills.

CLIMBING MORE RUNGS

There is no hard-and-fast rule regarding the number of times to do an exposure before you move on to the next rung. I suggest you do enough so you can comfortably be in that trigger situation without doing any avoidance or safety behaviors going forward. This will be confirmed by decreases in your SUDS and BIP ratings, which show that you're learning from your exposure experiments.

As you increase your comfort level in a particular situation, change up the context in which you do each exposure. For example, suppose your current rung is making eye contact and saying hey to some of your peers. After you've done that exposure in one setting, do it in some different settings. If you started by doing it in the hall at the beginning of school, now do it during recess, at lunch, before a class, after a class, when you depart for the day, and so on.

After you've done your first exposure experiment enough times to feel pretty comfortable, it's time to graduate to the next rung. Go back to the ladder you are working on and take a look at the next rung. Before you start with this new rung, reassess your SUDS rating for that rung. It's probably gotten lower as a result of the learning you achieved by doing exposures for the first rung. In fact, the next rung may now feel too easy. In that case, you can adjust the rungs on your ladder. Feel free to combine rungs if you want to take on a greater challenge in your next set of exposures. Remember, you're in charge of the challenges you want to take on!

Continue to climb the rungs on this ladder. After you've completed all the rungs on that ladder, you will be ready to plan your next exposure ladder. Return to your index cards and select the situation that is next lowest on your trigger situations list. Then repeat the process.

You don't have to follow the order you originally set up on your index cards. If it makes more sense to you now to pick a different trigger situation, do so. Again, you're in charge. The most important thing is to keep up your momentum. Do exposures regularly, every day if possible. Once you're on a roll, it will be easier to keep going than if you stop for several days.

Exposure Ideas

Creating exposures demands creativity. To get your creative juices flowing, here are some ideas for exposure experiments in various common trigger situations. These ideas target many fear structures. Some will apply to you and others not so much. You will know which apply based on the trigger situations you have identified. Test them out imaginally to see which might be useful to you.

Situation	Exposure ideas
Participating in the classroom	Ask a question.
	Answer a question.
	Volunteer to read aloud.
	Write on the whiteboard.
	Ask a teacher to repeat something.
	Ask a teacher for extra help.
	Ask a teacher for a letter of recommendation or reference.
Expressing opinions or preferences	Give your opinion about a book, song, sport, class, movie, or video game.
	Disagree with a friend even if they don't back down.
	Suggest an activity, place to eat, or movie to watch.
	Disagree with a suggestion ("I'd rather go for tacos than burgers").
	Express positive and negative feelings toward a friend ("I had so much fun when..." "I was bummed when you couldn't make it for...").

Situation	Exposure ideas
Interacting with peers (not just friends)	Invite someone to do homework together after school.
	Invite someone to attend a sporting event.
	Hang out after a sport or music practice and talk with peers.
	Smile and say hi to other kids.
	Make eye contact, smile, and say hi to other kids.
	Start a conversation in the hallway, before class, or after school.
	Post on social media.
	Attend a party.
	Host a party.
	Go to a school dance.
Making requests	Ask a peer for directions.
	Ask a peer for the time or date.
	Ask a peer for lecture notes.
	Ask a peer for a favor.
Being the center of attention	Drop something on purpose.
	Enter the classroom a tiny bit late.
	Yell across campus to a friend.
	Laugh extra loud.
	Spill something on purpose.

Situation	Exposure ideas
Additional ideas	Return an item to a store.
	Make a request for additional sizes or colors of something in a store.
	Make phone calls to ask about store hours or location, or make an appointment.
	Make phone calls in front of others.
	Eat in front of others.
	Write or type in front of others.
	Text in front of others.
	Use the restroom when others outside your stall can hear (bring water and pour it into the toilet to make more noise).
	Blow your nose in front of others.
	Wear an article of clothing slightly askew or with a spot on it.

Exposures to Bodily Sensations of Anxiety

In chapter 6, we talked about doing exposures to the bodily sensations of anxiety. These are also called *interoceptive exposures*. Because I wanted to keep things as simple as possible as you did your first exposures, I didn't include examples of this specific type in earlier chapters. Let's look more closely now at when and how you can do these exposures.

Identify your bodily sensations. Your first task is to identify which bodily sensations you fear and why. To do this, think about the last time you felt extremely anxious in a social situation. Ask yourself: *What bodily sensations, if any, do I feel when anxious? What do I fear about these sensations?* Use the downward arrow technique to determine what you fear about these sensations.

Here's a list of some common bodily sensations that can help you with this task:

- Sweating
- Hyperventilation
- Blushing
- Dizziness
- Trembling
- Heart palpitations

Do hyperventilation exercises. After you've identified the sensations you fear, you're going to try to intentionally bring them on. As with any other type of exposure, this is done so your brain can learn to be less fearful. In this case, it's learning to be less fearful of your bodily sensations of anxiety.

By far the most effective means to bring on any of the bodily sensations of anxiety is to hyperventilate (breathe too fast) on purpose. Hyperventilating on purpose is not dangerous. This is the method I use 99 percent of the time with teens. So, even if your sensations are just blushing or sweating, this is what I recommend you try.

Note: you should be in good health to do this exercise. If you suffer from asthma, seizures, or cardiac problems, check with your doctor before doing intentional hyperventilation.

Be prepared to work hard on this exercise. It should feel like a workout! As with all exposures, refrain from engaging in avoidance or safety behaviors. For example, don't reassure yourself by saying, "This is just an exercise, it's not real." Let yourself experience the sensations as much as possible, without stopping before the allotted time is up.

Here is what to do in your first session:

1. Breathe deeply and quickly through your mouth, using as much force as you can for a 15-second trial run.

2. After a pause, increase the time to 30 seconds.

3. After another pause, if you can tolerate it, increase the time to 60 seconds.

In subsequent sessions, after you have worked up to 60 seconds, you can just do the third step. Do 60 seconds, pause and breathe normally, and then do another 60 seconds. Two or three rounds of 60 seconds each usually works. But let your comfort level be your guide.

After each breathing session, ask yourself three questions: *Which bodily sensations did I experience? How similar is this to what I feel when anxious?* (Rate this on a scale of 1 to 10, with 10 indicating that the sensations are exactly alike.) *What is my SUDS rating?*

Expect some elevation in your SUDS rating initially. As you do more sessions, it will go down. If you can produce bodily sensations very close to what you feel when anxious in real life, you'll learn a lot from these exposures.

Try alternatives to hyperventilation exercises. Not everyone is able to produce bodily sensations through hyperventilation that are similar to what happens for them in real-life anxiety. If this is the case for you, this type of exposure won't help you much.

Fortunately, there are other ways to bring on the bodily sensations of anxiety. These include running in place and running upstairs. Follow the instructions for hyperventilation, but instead of breathing fast, run in place (or upstairs) for the allotted time. Then ask yourself the same set of questions.

You can also do interoceptive exposures that target fears of sensations such as blushing, shaking, and sweating. Here are some suggestions to produce these sensations:

- Sit close to a heater.
- Sit in a hot room wrapped in a blanket.
- Consume a hot liquid rapidly (careful not to burn your mouth or throat).
- Do push-ups.
- Hold weights in your outstretched arms.

If you have concerns about others noticing that you are sweating or blushing, you can add in vivo exposures. Before a social interaction, do one of the following:

- Mist yourself with a spray bottle to look like you are sweating.
- Apply makeup, such as strong blush, to your face to mimic blushing.

SOCIAL SKILLS BUILDING

If you suffer from social anxiety, you've probably avoided many social and performance situations. Doing this has made it harder to develop the know-how you need to have successful social interactions and relationships. Doing the CBT process presented in this book will help with that. But there's more you can do to build your skills.

Here are some tips on how to start a conversation, how to make small talk, how to keep a conversation going, how to switch topics, and how to extend an invitation. You will also learn about assertiveness skills, including nonverbal communication, expressing preferences, saying no, and sharing your feelings.

How to Start a Conversation

Let's start with how to identify good opportunities for conversations. When do you think would be a good time to start a conversation? Think about a typical time of day when you're around your peers. You may already have considered these types of situations while planning and carrying out your exposures:

- Before or after class, sports practice, or an assembly
- While waiting for a class or assembly to start
- During a warmup or cooldown in sports practice
- While in line for lunch
- While seated next to a peer in the cafeteria
- While waiting for a bus or when on the bus
- Any time you are physically near someone

Now consider what to say after you've identified a good opportunity for conversation. You can start by saying something simple. This type of conversation starter is called an *ice breaker*. An effective ice breaker is a comment or a question that gets others talking. It's most helpful when the topic is about something you have in common with the other person. For example:

"That history exam was tough."

"What did you think of the physics lab?"

"Did you finish the homework?"

"Wow, it's hot out here today!"

"Which topic did you pick for the paper?"

"That's a cool scarf. I've been looking for one like it."

"What are you having for lunch?"

Making Small Talk

After you've broken the ice, what do you say next? You make *small talk*. Small talk is polite but unimportant conversation about neutral topics, such as the weather, a homework assignment, or an experience you may have in common. Neither you nor the other person wants or expects the conversation to go very deep or last very long. It's just a way to feel more comfortable in the presence of others.

Here is a simple formula for teens who want to develop the art of small talk:

1. Ask a question.

2. Listen to the answer.

3. Ask another question related to the response.

4. Repeat steps 2 and 3.

Keep repeating these steps, each time asking a new question related to the previous response.

One tip for keeping the small talk going is to ask open-ended questions rather than ones that can be answered with a yes or no. You might start with a yes-or-no question to select a topic and then keep it going with open-ended questions. See how this works for Toby:

Toby: Did you go to choir practice yesterday? [yes-or-no question]

Chris: Yeah.

Toby: What songs did you all sing? [open-ended question]

Chris: We went through everything for the spring concert.

Toby: How did it sound? [open-ended question]

Chris: It sounded surprisingly good, actually. Except for the final song.

Toby: Oh? What went wrong with the last one? [open-ended question]

Chris: People didn't even remember the words. If you come today, I bet we'll do better. You have a strong voice and always know the words. You being there might help kids who don't have the words down.

Toby: Thanks. I'll see you there.

Switching Topics

You can only make small talk about something for so long before you'll need to change the subject. You may worry that switching topics will be difficult because you won't know what to say.

Keep in mind that a conversation involves at least two people. It's not your sole responsibility to carry on the conversation. The person with whom you're talking will have things to contribute. They may even change the topic before you have a chance to. But if they don't, look for these good times to switch topics: when you and the other person have nothing more to say about a topic, or when there is a long pause.

Keep in mind that awkward silences in social interactions are normal. Sometimes a conversation will naturally continue on the same or a related topic after a pause. Other times, a silence means it's a good time to switch topics. If you decide to switch topics, you can use the small talk formula. For example, instead of Toby ending his conversation with Chris, he could have responded as follows:

Chris: ... You being there might help kids who don't have the words down.

Toby: Thanks. [pause] Have you done the math homework yet? [yes-or-no question]

Chris: No.

Toby: How long do you think it will take? [open-ended question]

Chris: I don't know. The last one took an hour. I'm going to try to start it before choir practice.

Toby: It looks like it's going to be hard!

If a conversation has come to its natural end, nothing more needs to be said. If that seems to be the case, you can simply say something like, "Well, see you later in History," and walk away. There are no social rules about this. People have things to do, places to go, and so do you.

Invite Someone to Do Something with You

As you practice making small talk, you will feel more and more comfortable interacting with others. You'll learn that what counts is not so much *what* you say as the simple fact that you are interacting and connecting with others.

How do you connect more with others? By spending time with them! Extending and accepting invitations is an important way to ensure you do that. And those invitations, in turn, will lead to more meaningful friendships.

Most teens with social anxiety avoid extending invitations because they worry the person they invite will say no. If the person says yes, then they worry the person was only being polite and doesn't really want to do anything with them. (This is an example of the thinking error of mind reading.) To ease into making invitations, I recommend you start with a suggestion. As you did in making small talk, stay away from straight-up yes-or-no questions. For example:

Yes-or-no invitation: "Would you like to get together?"

Better: "Maybe we can get together sometime."

Yes-or-no invitation: "Do you want to study at the library?"

Better: "Maybe we could study this at the library together sometime."

When you extend an invitation, you will get one of three responses: positive, neutral, or negative.

- **Positive.** A positive response would be something like, "That would be great. Thanks." If you receive a positive response, you'll need to respond with a specific plan and exchange contact information. For example, "How about we go to the café Saturday afternoon to study? Let me get your number so I can text you about specifics later."

- **Neutral.** A neutral response might be just "Maybe." If you receive a neutral response, you can give a neutral response back. For example, "Okay." Then give it some time. If you feel you're getting to know the person a bit better, you can try another invitation in the future. Remember, there are many possible explanations for a neutral response to an invitation. The other kid may be shy or may simply be preoccupied with other things in the moment.

- **Negative.** A negative response would be something like, "No, I don't have time. Sorry." In this case, I suggest you end the conversation and walk away. It might sting a bit. But you can still pat yourself on the back for making the effort and trying something uncomfortable. Good job!

Assertiveness Skills

Communicating assertively means you are direct and honest in expressing your thoughts, feelings, and needs, while respecting the rights and needs of others. Being assertive is not the same as being rude or aggressive. Many teens with social anxiety struggle with communicating assertively. This limits the depth and quality of the relationships they have with others.

If you worry that expressing your thoughts, preferences, and feelings will lead to rejection, you won't learn how to develop meaningful and mutually rewarding relationships.

Here are some ways to practice this important set of skills. You can also make the practice of these skills part of your exposure ladders.

Use nonverbal communication. How you carry yourself physically is a language in and of itself. You can use it to feel and appear more assertive. Maintaining eye contact, standing up straight, and facing the person you are talking to are ways you can appear more assertive. Start small and build on your skills. For example, if making eye contact carries a higher SUDS rating than standing tall, start with standing tall.

Express your preferences. If you struggle with expressing your preferences due to fears others won't like what you say, they may think you don't have preferences. They may see you as indecisive if you don't share what you like and dislike. Your opinions are important to others. Sharing your thoughts is how you form social relationships, both deep and at the acquaintance level. If expressing your preferences triggers a SUDS rating, you'll need to practice until you feel more comfortable.

Using "I" statements (sentences that begin with "I") to express your preferences is helpful. For example, you might say, "I like Janelle Monáe's music. Do you?" Or "I like Pete's Pizzeria. Which pizza place do you like best?" Or "I like studying at the student center best."

It's okay to say no. You may worry that if you refuse to do something another person requests, that person will get angry, be disappointed, or have a low opinion of you. Have you ever agreed to do something you really didn't feel comfortable doing? It may feel easier in the moment to agree, but you may regret it later.

To practice this skill, you can say, "I'm sorry, but…" Then briefly say why you cannot or do not wish to do what was requested. If the person persists or begs you to do it, remain calm and say, "I'm sorry, I can't." I suggest you practice this skill before a mirror while imagining the scenario.

Share how you feel. If you have social anxiety, expressing your feelings may be the hardest part of learning to be more assertive. For example, you might worry that if you give a compliment, others will think you are nerdy, clingy, or "trying too hard." The problem with not sharing how you feel is that you can miss out on a shared positive experience.

Because no one can read the mind of another, this skill is important. How, for instance, is Joe supposed to know you were offended by a comment he made about your ethnicity if you don't tell him? How is Sarah to know you think her outfit looks cool if you don't tell her?

This skill isn't necessarily about sharing deep feelings with others. Being able to share anger, sadness, and disappointment—feelings everyone experiences at some point—is important for developing relationships. I suggest you start with simple feelings and compliments. When you're comfortable with easier feelings, you can move on from there.

FAQS

Q: *Isn't being assertive too pushy and bossy?*

A: The word "assertive" can have different meanings for different people. In this book it's about what you want, your preferences, your beliefs, and your opinions, as well as what you don't want, like, or believe. Being assertive doesn't mean being overpowering or domineering.

Now, not everyone will agree with your opinions, preferences, and desires. And if they did, the world would be very boring! Sharing with others what makes you tick forms the basis of friendships and relationships. We are all social creatures who are curious and want to know about one another.

Q: *If I just acted better and smarter, people would like me. Shouldn't I try to be better at everything?*

A: Researchers once did a study about what makes us attractive to others. The subjects listened to recordings of people answering questions: some answered perfectly, while others didn't answer well. One of those who answered perfectly also made a clumsy and embarrassing blunder—spilling coffee on his new suit! At the end, the subjects had to rate who was most likable. Who do you think it was?

I'll give you a hint: it's not who most teens with social anxiety would expect. It was not the person who did everything perfectly. The most liked was the one who performed well but also made mistakes. This is known as the *pratfall effect:* someone who makes a few blunders is more attractive than someone who comes across as a superhero. So being perfectly smart or witty in all conversations is not what will make people like you. They'd rather see that you're willing to be yourself, take risks, and show some weakness.

Q: *Is social distancing helpful for social anxiety?*

A: Now that we know what it's like to live in a world where people have been asked to practice social distancing—and may be asked to do it again in the future—that's a valuable question. You may have noticed that you feel immediate relief when you socially distance. That's because social distancing keeps you out of your trigger situations. In fact, it can seem like a green light to use your avoidance and safety behaviors. However, social distancing also stops you from being able to run exposure experiments.

Although social distancing may seem helpful for social anxiety, it's not. The difference is that, unlike avoidance and safety behaviors, sometimes you need to socially distance for your own or others' health, or both. Just be aware that whenever a period of recommended social distancing ends, your anxiety may increase. That's a good time to start (or resume) exposures.

Q: *I don't think anyone really wants to get to know me. Won't I feel worse if I try being more social?*

A: The power of our thoughts is very strong. If you believe others simply don't care to know you, then of course you will have difficulty considering the possibility that other kids might like you if given a chance. I suggest you create some exposure experiments for the specific situations that trigger this belief. This way you can learn whether you are correct in your belief that others don't want to know you. If you avoid interacting with others as much as possible, you won't have a chance to disprove your beliefs.

Your exposures can involve gradually reducing your avoidance. For example, you might decide to make eye contact and say hi. Then look for objective evidence to support your prediction of what will happen. How will you know for sure a person doesn't want to know you? How many people have to ignore you for you to feel worse for trying? Keep track of the evidence and see what happens when you reduce your avoidance.

CHAPTER 11

How Well Are You Doing?

Doing exposures requires discipline, courage, and the ability to focus on the scientific model. You are following this exposure-based program because you know it's effective. Still, it helps to keep your eye on the prize. If you feel discouraged, ask yourself, *Why am I doing this?* Your answer: *To feel more confident and comfortable in the social situations I want to be in!*

REVIEW YOUR PROGRESS

Progress and motivation go hand in hand. When you see your progress, you feel more motivated to continue. In addition, reviewing the progress you make every day, every week, and beyond will help you hold yourself accountable.

Daily Progress

Check in with yourself daily. Are you resisting doing these behaviors 100 percent of the time while in trigger situations? If not, when are you slipping? It may not be realistic to expect 100 percent, especially during your first exposures. When you slip, don't beat yourself up. Try to figure out what happened and get back on track.

Hopefully you're doing exposures several times a day. Be sure to fill out both Before and After the Exposure Worksheets each time. Your responses give you good data about your progress. Please don't skip answering the question "What did I learn?" after each exposure and before you plan new exposures. Answering it helps consolidate the new learning your brain has achieved by doing exposures.

In fact, I recommend you take the data a step further by making a habit of recording them in log form. You can use a notebook or tablet, and draw a line down the middle of each page. On the left, put your before-exposure data: both the percentage you believed your prediction would be correct and your estimated SUDS rating. On the right, put your after-exposure data: the percentage you believe it now and your actual SUDS rating.

Here is what Diya's log looked like after several exposure experiments:

	Before		After	
Exposure 1	BIP 60%	SUDS 4	BIP 10%	SUDS 3
Exposure 2	BIP 100%	SUDS 5	BIP 20%	SUDS 4
Exposure 3	BIP 50%	SUDS 3	BIP 2%	SUDS 2

Weekly Progress

If you keep a log of exposures with your data points and dates of exposures, you will be able to see your progress over time. You want to see reductions in both the percentage you believe feared outcomes will happen and your SUDS ratings. Because you are moving on to new exposure ladders, you may miss the progress you are making. Also, during your early exposures, things may feel harder before they get easier. Keeping track of your data anchors you in objectivity rather than emotion. Objective numbers offer powerful and convincing evidence of your progress.

Monthly Progress and Beyond

Of course, everyone goes at their own pace when doing exposures. You may feel so great after one month of exposures that you decide you've met your goals. Or you may go slower and work on exposures over several months. All that matters is that you move forward until you can be in trigger situations without doing avoidance or safety behaviors.

When you think you're ready to stop doing formal exposures, sit down and review your data. It can be easy to forget how hard something was after it has become easy. You may be making more progress than you realize. Looking at your data will tell you exactly where you stand. This will also motivate you to take the steps needed to maintain the gains you've made.

MAINTAIN YOUR GAINS

You've worked hard to increase your comfort in social situations, so it's important to maintain those gains. And those gains will help you handle other trigger situations that may arise in the future. Your life will undoubtedly present new potential trigger situations. You may go to college, get a job, eventually have a career, meet many new people, date someone, and so on. Your vulnerability to anxiety won't go away. So let's talk about how to stay on top of your anxiety so it doesn't have the chance to grow again.

Keep training your mind. Even after you finish formal exposures, stay mentally limber in trigger situations by practicing doing exposures. I suggest making a list of trigger situations that have been hardest for you or that don't occur frequently, and select two or three to do each week. Do this on an ongoing basis.

You can think of this work as being similar to how athletes maintain fitness during off-seasons. They need to maintain their strength and stamina to manage the more intensive training they'll be called upon to do in the next season. As a competitive athlete since I was a teen, I know this well. Once, after an injury, I stopped training between seasons. Boy, did I learn a painful lesson! The first six weeks after I started training again were torture. Also, I was more prone to injury without that base of training. After that experience, I never let my fitness go to zero again.

Don't be rattled if your SUDS rating is higher than you expected on a given day. View it as a signal that you need to stay fit. Don't get down on yourself about it. Just call it what it is and get back on track, using the knowledge you have gained in this book. You understand how anxiety works: what feeds it, what maintains it, and how to conquer it. Once you know how to use the CBT process, you have the skills to manage anxiety and maintain your gains for the rest of your life.

Hold yourself accountable with self-compassion. Some days will be easier than others. One day you might feel triggered a lot and your anxiety might feel more intense than on another day. This is the nature of all anxiety problems: they wax and wane. Every person who does exposures will face these dynamics, and it helps to remind yourself that this is normal.

Similarly, sometimes it will feel easier than other times to stick with the program. That is to be expected. For example, if you deal with mood problems, such as feeling depressed, your anxiety will likely seem worse when you feel depressed. Hormones can also play a role. For example, most women who suffer from anxiety experience a worsening of symptoms during premenstrual phases of their cycle.

Rather than getting harsh with yourself for not meeting the goals you set or for faltering, try to show yourself some compassion. One way to express self-compassion is to take the role of a good friend with yourself. How would a good friend advise you? Would a friend berate you and say you'll never make progress? Of course not! A friend would listen to you and empathize with your feelings and try to help you problem solve. When a friend isn't around, be that friend for yourself!

Be aware of signs of relapse. Ask yourself, *What would I notice first if my social anxiety was getting worse again?* Probably the answer is that you'd notice an increase in avoidance behaviors. Given that avoidance behaviors aren't always obvious, even to you, it's a good idea to troubleshoot ahead of time. What would that avoidance look like? Be honest with yourself. Accept that the emotion of anxiety is strong and can trick you into excuses that seem reasonable. For example, you might tell yourself, *I just don't feel up to it today.* Or *I have too much homework.* Or *I'll go next time.*

What if you relapse? First, I want you to be aware that if you *fear* a relapse—and if you try to push anxious thoughts or sensations out of mind to avoid it—you're more likely to actually relapse. The best attitude to have is an accepting one: accept that your mind may get stuck on particular fears in the future and that you have the tools, strategies, and experience to manage whatever comes your way.

Chances are, you will be in situations that trigger anxiety about being judged by others again. Being triggered does not necessarily mean you are relapsing. How you respond to being triggered determines whether you relapse or not. If you resume avoidance or safety behaviors when you are triggered in the future, you will likely relapse. If you resist those behaviors and practice the skills you have, you will not go back to square one.

GETTING THE SUPPORT YOU NEED

Other students. Consider sharing this book with your peers. Together, you can organize to promote mental health among students, such as through a club, a column in the school newspaper, or being mental health ambassadors. You aren't alone! There is much less stigma these days than there used to be about mental health issues. Young people such as yourself are learning that our minds are just as likely as our bodies to be affected by problems. In fact, it is becoming a source of honor and altruism to care for the emotional well-being of others.

Your parents. Of course, your parents want to help you conquer your fears. However, they may not understand how to help. In addition, you may not want to confide in your parents about your anxiety. Perhaps you feel embarrassed to admit that you have anxiety about situations you know many of your peers or even siblings don't. Maybe your parents don't listen to you, or they make you feel bad about your fears. Maybe your parents suffer from their own anxieties, have a hard time seeing you distressed, and hence participate in avoidance and safety behaviors with you.

Despite all the reasons you may have not to, I suggest you share with your parents what you have learned in this book. They can read it as well. If they have been participating in avoidance and safety behaviors with you, reading this book will help them see that those actions feed and maintain your anxiety. I've provided some additional resources for parents at the end of this book.

Counselors or therapists. Share this book with your school counselor or your individual therapist if you see one. Since there is a shortage of professionals trained in CBT, despite its well-known track record, most need to be educated to help you. Please don't let a mental health practitioner not solidly trained in CBT convince you that you must address "deeper issues" or "trauma" to overcome your social anxiety. This is an uninformed and old-fashioned stance, which many mental health professionals unfortunately still follow. Without expertise in CBT, it is unlikely that such a therapist will be able to help you.

When to seek professional help. Social anxiety exists on a continuum. We all have a bit of it. At some point, everyone has a concern about being judged negatively and perhaps even rejected. No one likes to feel embarrassed or feel the physiological sensations of anxiety to the extent that we worry others will notice and think less of us. Some people will suffer at a relatively mild level and be able to resist avoidance and safety behaviors with relative ease. Others will suffer more: their distress will be higher and they will have a harder time resisting avoidance and safety behaviors.

You may need the support of a trained CBT clinician if you find you cannot follow this program due to intense anxiety. You also may need professional help if you don't make progress due to factors such as family stressors or coexisting issues that make following a program like this difficult. This does not mean you can't overcome your social anxiety. It just means you need additional support. Many reputable organizations specialize in helping people of all ages with anxiety and related problems. Check out the list of resources provided at the end of this book.

There are also safe and effective medicines that can help you. The serotonin reuptake inhibitors (SSRI) are safe and effective for teens to take for social anxiety. When taking such medicines, exposures tend to feel more manageable and avoidance and safety behaviors become easier to resist. For this, you will need to schedule a consultation with a psychiatrist. Most CBT clinicians can help you find an appropriate psychiatrist. Medications should be used in conjunction with CBT for best results. Virtual-reality (VR) exposures are a new field that may provide help in the future.

SUMMING IT UP

Now that you've learned all the basics about the CBT Social Anxiety Relief Program, you have what you need for success! Hopefully, you already have some exposures under your belt and are beginning to get the hang of it and seeing some results.

This may be the end of the book, but it's the beginning of your work to face your anxieties so that they lose their power over you. Keep cycling through the five steps of the program:

1. Create a trigger situations list.

2. Identify avoidance and safety behaviors.

3. Build an exposure ladder.

4. Run an exposure experiment.

5. Climb more rungs on the ladder.

Refer back to the instructions and examples in this book frequently, especially when you feel stuck or are facing a new trigger situation. The same principles will always apply. Go back to basics if you feel challenged. You will quickly find your way again. Resist becoming overwhelmed by anxious emotions or thinking there is something else wrong with you. You can do this if you just keep at it!

Resources

1. The following organizations have a "find a therapist" function to help you locate a clinician in your area:

    Anxiety and Depression Association of America, https://adaa.org

    Association for Behavioral and Cognitive Therapies, https://www.abct.org

2. For more general information about social anxiety check out:

    National Institute of Mental Health, https://www.nimh.nih.gov/health/statistics/social-anxiety-disorder.shtml

3. For parents:

    Lebowitz, E. R. 2019. *Addressing Parental Accommodation When Treating Anxiety in Children* (ABCT Clinical Practice Series). New York, NY: Oxford University Press.

    Walker, B. 2017. *Anxiety Relief for Kids: On-the-Spot Strategies to Help Your Child Overcome Worry, Panic, and Avoidance.* Oakland, CA: New Harbinger.

References

Abramowitz, J. S., J. B. Deacon, and S. P. H. Whiteside. 2019. *Exposure Therapy for Anxiety, Second Edition: Principles and Practice*. New York, NY: The Guilford Press.

Aronson, E., B. Willerman, & J. Floyd. 1966. "The Effect of a Pratfall on Increasing Interpersonal Attractiveness." *Psychonomic Science*, 4(6): 227–228.

Craske, M. G., M. Treanor, C. Conway, T. Zbozinek, and B. Vervliet. 2015. "Maximizing Exposure Therapy: An Inhibitory Learning Approach." *Behaviour Research and Therapy*, 58, 10–23. doi: 10.1016/j.brat.2014.04.006

Du Maurier, D. 1938. *Rebecca*. Garden City, NY: Doubleday.

Fritscher, L. 2020. "Social Anxiety Disorder Information." https://www.verywellmind.com/what-is-social-phobia-2671698#citation-5

Leigh, E., and David M. Clark. 2018. "Understanding Social Anxiety Disorder in Adolescents and Improving Treatment Outcomes: Applying the Cognitive Model of Clark and Wells (1995)." *Clinical Child and Family Psychology Review*. 21(3): 388–414.

Sundaram, J. 2019. "Genetic Risk Associated with Social Anxiety." *News Medical*. https://www.news-medical.net/health/Genetic-Risk-Associated-with-Social-Anxiety.aspx.

Bridget Flynn Walker, PhD, is a licensed clinical psychologist specializing in the assessment and treatment of individuals with anxiety and related disorders. She is a graduate of the University of California, Berkeley; and earned her doctorate in clinical psychology at California School of Professional Psychology in Berkeley, CA. She has particular expertise using cognitive behavioral therapy (CBT) with anxious children and adolescents and their families. She is author of *Anxiety Relief for Kids*, which enjoys international readership and has been selected as an Association for Behavioral and Cognitive Therapies Self-Help Book Recommendation—an honor bestowed on outstanding self-help books that are consistent with CBT principles, and that incorporate scientifically tested strategies for overcoming mental health difficulties.

Walker has trained doctoral-level clinicians in CBT and anxiety disorders. In addition, mental health professionals throughout the San Francisco Bay Area request her consultation and teaching services. She is a lecturer at the University of California at San Francisco-Osher Mini Medical School, and is frequently asked to educate and guide school professionals in the San Francisco Bay Area and nationally. She is known for her skill at making CBT clear and accessible to nonprofessionals. She lives in San Francisco, CA. Visit her at www.drbridgetwalker.com.

Foreword writer **Michael A. Tompkins, PhD, ABPP**, is author of *My Anxious Mind: A Teen's Guide to Managing Anxiety and Panic*. He is codirector of the San Francisco Bay Area Center for Cognitive Therapy; and assistant clinical professor of psychology at the University of California, Berkeley.

More Instant Help Books for Teens
An Imprint of New Harbinger Publications

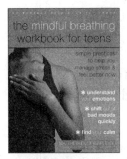

THE MINDFUL BREATHING WORKBOOK FOR TEENS
Simple Practices to Help You Manage Stress and Feel Better Now
978-1684037247 / US $17.95

CONQUER NEGATIVE THINKING FOR TEENS
A Workbook to Break the Nine Thought Habits That Are Holding You Back
978-1626258891 / US $17.95

THE TEEN GIRL'S SURVIVAL GUIDE
Ten Tips for Making Friends, Avoiding Drama, and Coping with Social Stress
978-1626253063 / US $17.95

PUT YOUR WORRIES HERE
A Creative Journal for Teens with Anxiety
978-1684032143 / US $17.95

THE GROWTH MINDSET WORKBOOK FOR TEENS
Say Yes to Challenges, Deal with Difficult Emotions, and Reach Your Full Potential
978-1684035571 / US $18.95

THE SELF-ESTEEM WORKBOOK FOR TEENS
Activities to Help You Build Confidence and Achieve Your Goals
978-1608825820 / US $17.95

newharbingerpublications
1-800-748-6273 / newharbinger.com
(VISA, MC, AMEX / prices subject to change without notice)   Follow Us

Don't miss out on new books in the subjects that interest you.
Sign up for our Book Alerts at **newharbinger.com/bookalerts**

Did you know there are free tools you can download for this book?

Free tools are things like **worksheets, guided meditation exercises**, and **more** that will help you get the most out of your book.

You can download free tools for this book—whether you bought or borrowed it, in any format, from any source—from the **New Harbinger** website. All you need is a NewHarbinger.com account. Just use the URL provided in this book to view the free tools that are available for it. Then, click on the "download" button for the free tool you want, and follow the prompts that appear to log in to your NewHarbinger.com account and download the material.

You can also save the free tools for this book to your **Free Tools Library** so you can access them again anytime, just by logging in to your account! Just look for this button on the book's free tools page:

> + save this to my
> free tools library

If you need help accessing or downloading free tools, visit **newharbinger.com/faq** or contact us at customerservice@newharbinger.com.